Published by Hyndman Publishing
325 Purchas Road
RD 2 Amberley 7482

ISBN: 1-877382-55-8

TEXT: © Simon & Alison Holst

DESIGN: Rob Di Leva

PHOTOGRAPHER: Lindsay Keats

HOME ECONOMISTS: Simon & Alison
Holst, Michelle Gill

FOOD STYLIST: Simon Holst

STYLING & PROPS: Pip Spite

Introduction

What could be more inviting than the wonderful aroma of freshly baked bread? We have enjoyed making bread for our own satisfaction and for our families, for many years.

We still get excited about the fact that, using only a few humble and inexpensive ingredients, we can produce exciting breads which will turn the simplest meal into something really special. What's more, it's nice to know that a loaf of home-made bread is good for us all, and for our families, since it has great flavour, is high in good, complex carbohydrates, and low in fat. And last but not least, making your own bread saves you money, too!

Many years ago, Alison couldn't believe her eyes, as a student at the University of Otago's Home Science School, when she saw how to make and bake bread rolls of all shapes and sizes in the Food Laboratory. A few years later, when she was teaching young women in the same laboratory, she found that her students were every bit as excited by the process of bread-making as she had been. Simon, a generation later, graduated from the University of Canterbury and his first job was as a food scientist in a bread laboratory. Because of this background, and his inquiring mind, he is a wonderful bread maker.

Over the years we have thoroughly enjoyed working with bread. At first we mixed, then kneaded various loaves by hand, shaping them, watching them rise, then baking them in our own kitchens.

Not too long after this, we watched with great excitement and some disbelief while a wonderful new invention, the bread machine, did all the mixing, kneading and baking for us. All we had to do was measure our ingredients into the container, shut the lid, and turn on the machine. Magic!

Recently we have experimented with "no knead" bread – made by hand, with very little effort in just a few minutes, which, as the name suggests, requires no kneading at all!

Last but not least we have added sections on 'Baking Powder Breads' and 'Gluten-free' bread. The former are "quick breads", risen by baking powder rather than yeast, and can be mixed and baked in a short time.

Gluten-free foods are important for an increasing number of people. We are delighted with our gluten-free breads that look and taste delicious.

Whether you are thinking about starting to make bread for the first time or are an experienced bread maker, we are sure you will really enjoy making bread from the different sections in this book, and that your families will share your pleasure and excitement in the results, as ours do.

Simon and Alison Holst, 2010

Contents

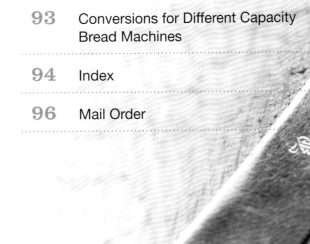

Using a bread machine

We think that bread machines are truly wonderful – almost too good to be true.

Fancy being able to measure a few basic ingredients into a machine, then pressing two or three buttons, and coming back a few hours later (or waking up in the morning) to remove a warm, fragrant, ready-to-eat loaf of bread!

This, however, is only part of the story. Throughout this book you will see photos of our breads. Some were made in a bread machine from scratch, while others were mixed, kneaded and risen in a machine, then taken out, shaped by hand, and baked in a regular oven.

To our way of thinking, the machine does all the rather messy and tedious work, leaving us the fun part, hand-shaping warm, satiny dough. When you use a bread machine in this way, you greatly increase the range and type of breads you can make. What's more, you won't think twice about making breads like pizza bases and pita breads on a regular basis.

People keep asking us if a bread machine is worth the initial investment. We think it is, as long as you use it regularly, and especially if you make hand-shaped and fancy breads that cost much more than regular basic loaves to buy. For example, when you make a dozen or so croissants or bagels, you can save $15–20 per batch.

Most modern machines are designed to make loaves using either 3 or 4 cups of flour (producing loaves weighing around 750g or 1kg respectively). We have based our recipes on 3 cups (420g) of flour, which we feel suits the majority of machines. Some older machines are designed to use about 2 cups of flour, in which case you can scale down our recipes (see the table on page 93). If your machine is bigger than the ones we use, you can scale the recipes up, or use them as they are.

The manufacturers of different machines suggest adding ingredients in different orders. Always follow their guidelines, especially if you are using the timer setting.

Some machines work best with slightly different liquid to flour ratios. Whenever you try a new recipe, be prepared to experiment a little, and make small changes if necessary. We find that the best way to ensure success is to always check the dough in its first few minutes of kneading. It is fun to watch the machine getting under way anyway, so don't be afraid to open the machine to take a look. Within 5 minutes, the dough should have formed an even round ball or cylinder that is not too sticky. If it looks too dry, add 1–2 tablespoons of water gradually. If it is too wet, add 1–2 tablespoons of flour. You will quickly learn which dough consistency gives the best results in your machine.

From time to time, you may find that you have trouble with your "tried and true" recipes. Don't be alarmed, read the instructions that came with your bread machine, and the suggestions on page 5 and try again. Remember that bread dough is a living thing, and its behaviour may be affected by many factors.

Bread machine tips

First, an important message from Alison. However excited you may be about the wonderful things a new machine will do, if you are a bit older and have trouble operating new gadgets you may be a bit daunted by the idea of getting a bread machine going! In the past I have found that the best way to learn about a new machine is to encourage my children to read the instructions and use the machine. I then get them to show me what to do, and operate it under their supervision, preferably several times (they need to be at least 10 years old). After this, I am "away laughing", can read and understand the instruction book, and can see just how simple the machine is.

If you are not completely familiar with your bread machine, you might try the same thing, borrowing a neighbour's child if necessary.

We hope that you will read all the pages in this book, including those without recipes, because they have been written to help you. Make sure you also read and reread the instructions that came with your bread machine — or whenever you have teething problems — because you are sure to learn some finer points each time. The manufacturer knows your particular machine better than we do, but these are answers we have found by trial and error.

Sunken top and/or collapsed middle?

Too much water — try 2 tablespoons less

Too much yeast — try ½ teaspoon less (the dough rises too quickly, then collapses before baking)

No salt, or too little salt (salt slows down yeast and "tightens" the dough)

The room temperature/humidity is too high — try a quick cycle

Coarse or holey texture?

Too much liquid — try 2 tablespoons less

Fermenting too quickly; try a short cycle

Room temperature too high

Too much sugar — use ½ teaspoon less

Uneven top?

Dough too stiff, not enough water — try adding 1–2 tablespoons

Small compact loaf or poor rising?

Too little yeast

No yeast. Did you forget it?

Yeast beyond expiry date

Measurement errors — not enough yeast or water, or too much salt

Dough too stiff — not enough water

Yeast has reacted with water too soon when using time delay – check the order in which ingredients should be added

If you are using the rapid cycle, try adding an extra ½ teaspoon of yeast and another teaspoon of sugar

We found that it was much easier to put ingredients in the bread machine bowl if we took the bowl out of the machine first.

One of the bonuses of bread machines is their delayed start (timer) function and the fact that they switch off at the completion of the cycle, but there are a few points to note about this including the fact that not all bread recipes are suitable for timer delay because of the ingredients they contain – we've noted these through the book. We've also found the bread is much nicer if removed from the machine as soon as possible at the end of the baking cycle. If you leave your loaf in the machine after baking is complete, the crust may become quite soggy and some loaves will shrink considerably.

Making bread by hand

Like many other people, we get a great deal of pleasure and satisfaction from making bread by hand.

Once you get into a bread-making routine, you will wonder why you ever considered it a complicated procedure. Although the whole process involves a number of steps, few of these are very time-consuming, and can mostly be fitted in between other activities.

Using your bread-making skills, you can start with a few basic, inexpensive ingredients, and some very simple equipment, and finish up with some spectacularly good bread, literally made with your own hands, of which you can be justifiably proud.

As you become an experienced bread maker, you will "get the feel of" the dough, adding flour, and other ingredients as necessary, rather than in fixed amounts, and using the amounts given in the recipe as a guide only. We are sure that once you know what you are doing, you will start changing our recipes, and developing your own specialties.

Don't try to produce bread identical to commercially made, light-textured, white sandwich bread, and don't expect your home-made breads to stay fresh for a week. Create instead unique bread made from interesting and different ingredients, and enjoy it hot from the oven, or at least within a couple of days.

After making all the recipes in this book by hand, often several times, we decided there are several pieces of invaluable equipment. The first of these is a timer – there is nothing worse than forgetting when your bread is ready for its next step!

1 Because the first few minutes of kneading a soft dough can be messy, we like to use a straight-sided plastic scraper to lift off the pieces of dough that stick to the work surface.

2 We think that a sturdy food mixer with a dough hook is a great help to anyone who makes hand-made bread regularly, although we know that some bread-makers will not agree with us. Using a dough hook will result in dough that is softer than you can achieve by hand, freeing you for 10 minutes to clean up or do other things.

3 One of the reasons bread machines make such good bread is that the process is timed and cannot be speeded up by impatient cooks. If you take shortcuts and hurry from one bread-making step to the next you are likely to have disappointing results.

The two most important processes are kneading and rising (see page 8). If you have a friend who makes bread, watch her or him kneading (since actions are better than words) then try it for yourself.

Our instructions give fairly specific rising times. These relate to good conditions (see page 9).

Although we know that you will be eager to eat your bread as soon as possible, remember that it will cut much better if you leave it for an hour or so to cool down. A really sharp bread knife is well worthwhile (page 96).

We hope that you will have fun making, sharing and eating the breads in this book.

Kneading and rising

Kneading

The best way to learn to knead bread is to watch an experienced bread maker kneading dough from the stage where it is turned out of its mixing bowl until it is smooth and satiny, does not stick to the working surface, and springs back when gently pressed with a finger.

To keep the dough as soft as possible, add no more flour than necessary, but use enough to stop it sticking to your hands and the bench. We recommend you knead it by pushing the dough down firmly, away from you, using the heel of one hand, then collect it with a circular movement of the other hand, bringing it back to the position where it can be pushed away again. The dough should travel more or less in a circle.

The dough hook of a strong electric mixer will knead bread dough efficiently, too. Dough hooks save time and energy if you intend to make hand-made bread regularly.

However you knead your dough, keep track of the time you spend (and use the time given in the recipe as a guide), since sufficient time and work is required to change the structure of the dough.

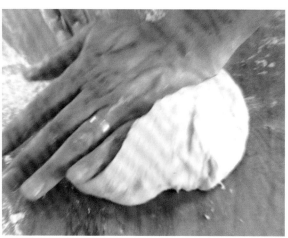

Rising Dough

Bread dough rises or increases in volume because it contains yeast, which grows and multiplies, producing bubbles of carbon dioxide that are trapped in the kneaded dough.

Yeast grows best when warm. When cold, it grows very slowly. If it gets too hot the culture will die, and the dough will never rise.

A place of just the right temperature (warmth) is therefore very important.

To keep a pocket of still, warm air above the yeast mixture while it is rising, we recommend covering the bowl of dough with cling film.

We find that the most reliable and successful places to rise doughs and loaves include a microwave oven and a conventional oven in which the bread will later be baked.

Microwave the cling film covered glass or plastic bowl of dough on Defrost (30% power) for 1 minute, at 5–10 minute intervals. Always check the dough temperature (it should feel warm, but not hot) before you microwave it again.

To warm conventional ovens for rising bread, heat a gas oven for 1 minute, and an electric oven for 2–3 minutes, at intervals. Check for warmth by putting your hand in the oven. Always remove the dough while heating the oven, so your bread cannot overheat if you are called away or have a memory lapse!

One of our favourite ways to rise dough is to heat the oven for a minute or two (as above), then place a baking pan or roasting dish on the bottom rack of the oven (at least 10cm below the rack where the dough will be rested) and then pour 2–3cm of very hot or boiling water into the baking pan. This helps keep the oven warm for a surprising length of time and increases the humidity.

After the risen bread is put in the oven to bake, it expands still further. We have found that it often expands more if it is baked without the fan on for the first 15 minutes.

Yeast can be bought in a number of different forms; the most readily available (from any supermarket) are dry forms. These are also easy and convenient to use, so these are what we've used in this book.

There are two major forms of dry yeast. Although either will work in any given recipe they will give slightly different results and are best suited to different types of bread. We have specified the type we think is best suited to each recipe.

Active Dried Yeast: this is beige coloured spherical yeast granules and contains no 'improvers'. Produces a loaf with a more open (larger bubbles) texture – great for 'hearth-style' breads.

Surebake Active Yeast: this is a mixture of beige yeast granules and fine white powder (a mixture of wheat flour, sugars, vitamins and other 'improvers'). Tends to produce a fine textured bread (good for 'sandwich-type' loaves). Produces a tighter (more elastic) dough that is a bit harder to roll out and shape.

Some home bakers also like to use compressed yeast. This can be used in place of instant active yeast (use 1 tablespoon of compressed yeast in place of 1¼ tsp of instant active yeast).

By Hand or
Bread Machine

Our Favourite White Bread

We find it enormously satisfying to make this delicious sweet-smelling, finely textured nicely risen white loaf.

Makes 1 large loaf (7–8 cup pan):

3 tsp Surebake yeast

1¼ cups plus 2 Tbsp warm water

2 Tbsp lecithin granules or oil

2 tsp sugar

1½ tsp salt

2 Tbsp non-fat milk powder

3 cups (420g) high-grade flour

Bread Machine Instructions

Carefully measure all the ingredients into a 750g capacity bread machine in the order specified by the manufacturer.

Set to the NORMAL/WHITE bread cycle, MEDIUM crust and START (or use the DOUGH cycle and shape and bake by hand). This is a very good timer bread.

Hand-made Bread Instructions

Measure the first six ingredients into a large bowl. Add 1½ cups of the measured flour and mix thoroughly. Cover and leave for 15 minutes or longer in a warm place.

Stir in the remaining flour, adding a little extra warm water or flour if necessary, to make a dough just firm enough to knead.

Knead with the dough hook of an electric mixer or by hand on a lightly floured surface for 10 minutes, adding extra flour if necessary, until the dough forms a soft ball that springs back when gently pressed.

Turn the dough in 2–3 teaspoons of oil in the cleaned dry bowl, cover with cling film and leave in a warm draught-free place for about 30 minutes.

Lightly knead the oiled dough in the bowl for 1 minute. Pat it into a square shape a little longer than the baking pan, then roll into a cylinder. Put into the sprayed or buttered bread pan, pressing it into the corners and levelling the top.

Leave to rise in a warm, draught-free place for about 1 hour or until double its original size.

If desired, brush with milk or egg glaze (page 87) and sprinkle with sesame seeds, then bake at 200°C for about 30 minutes or until the sides and bottom are browned and the loaf sounds hollow when tapped.

Wholemeal Bread

This recipe gives a good-sized loaf of traditional brown bread. Not only is it delicious, with the light texture children love, but it is also an excellent source of fibre. Use it for sandwiches or toast.

Makes 1 medium loaf (6–8 cup pan):

3 tsp Surebake yeast

1½ cups warm water

2 tsp sugar

1 tsp salt

2 Tbsp lecithin granules or oil

2 Tbsp gluten flour (page 91)

2 Tbsp non-fat milk powder (optional)

3 cups (420g) wholemeal flour

2 Tbsp wheat germ (optional)

Bread Machine Instructions

Carefully measure all the ingredients into a 750g capacity bread machine in the order specified by the manufacturer.

Set to the NORMAL/WHITE or WHOLE WHEAT cycle, MEDIUM crust and START. This is a good timer bread.

Hand-made Bread Instructions

Measure the first six ingredients plus milk powder, if using, into a large bowl, add 1½ cups of the wholemeal flour and mix thoroughly. Cover and leave for 15 minutes or longer in a warm place.

Stir in the remaining wholemeal flour, and wheat germ if using, and add a little extra flour if necessary to make a dough just firm enough to knead.

Knead with the dough hook of an electric mixer or by hand on a lightly floured surface for 10 minutes, adding extra flour if necessary, until the dough forms a soft ball that springs back when gently pressed.

Turn in 2–3 teaspoons of oil in the cleaned dry bowl, cover with cling film and leave in a warm draught-free place for 30–40 minutes.

Pat the dough into a square shape a little longer than the baking pan, then roll into a cylinder. Put into the sprayed or buttered bread pan, pressing it into the corners and levelling the top.

Leave to rise in a warm, draught-free place for about 1 hour or until double the original size.

Bake at 200°C for about 30 minutes or until the sides and bottom are browned and the loaf sounds hollow when tapped.

Cheese Muffin Bread

Bake this as a rich cheese loaf, top with grated cheese and cook like muffins in pans, or make novel pull-apart Monkey breads if you feel like something different.

Makes 1 large loaf, 12 muffin buns, or 2 x 18cm Monkey bread rings:

3 tsp Surebake yeast

¾ cup warm water

2 large eggs

2 Tbsp lecithin granules or butter

2 tsp sugar

1 tsp salt

2 Tbsp non-fat milk powder

3 cups (420g) high-grade flour

¾ cup grated tasty cheese

½ tsp chilli powder (optional)

melted butter

grated Parmesan or tasty cheese

milk

Bread Machine Instructions

Carefully measure the first eight ingredients into a 750g capacity bread machine in the order specified by the manufacturer.

Set to the NORMAL/WHITE bread cycle, MEDIUM crust and START (or use the dough cycle and shape and bake using the instructions given below).

Hand-made Bread Instructions

Measure the first seven ingredients into a large bowl with 1½ cups of high-grade flour and mix thoroughly. Cover and leave for 15 minutes or longer in a warm place.

Stir in the flour, cheese and the chilli powder, if using, and a little extra flour or water if necessary, to make a dough just firm enough to knead.

Knead with the dough hook of an electric mixer or by hand on a lightly floured surface for 10 minutes, adding extra flour if necessary, until the dough forms a soft ball that springs back when gently pressed.

Turn the dough in 2–3 teaspoons of oil in the cleaned dry bowl, cover with cling film and leave in a warm draught-free place for 30–40 minutes.

Lightly knead the dough in the bowl for 1 minute, then shape as desired.

Shaping

To make a loaf: shape as on page 88.

To make muffin buns: divide the dough into 12 pieces and roll into balls. Put into sprayed medium-size muffin pans and leave to rise in a warm draught-free place for 1 hour or until doubled in volume. Dampen tops with milk and sprinkle with grated tasty cheese. Bake at 220°C for 10–12 minutes until tops, sides and bottom are golden brown.

To make Monkey bread: divide the dough into four, then eight, then 16, then 32 equal-size pieces. Roll each ball in a little melted butter, then in grated Parmesan or tasty cheese. Line the bottom of two 20cm ring pans with baking paper and oil the sides. Put 16 of the cheesy balls evenly in each pan. Cover with cling film and leave to rise in a warm draught-free place for about 1 hour or until almost double in volume. Bake at 220°C for 15–20 minutes or until golden brown. Serve warm.

Mixed Grain Bread

Precooking the kibbled grains may seem a bit fiddly, but it ensures a moist loaf. The large, light-textured loaf, flecked with kibbled grains, is a just reward for the extra effort.

Makes 1 large loaf (8 cup pan):

½ cup (85g) mixed kibbled grains*

3 tsp Surebake yeast

1¼ cups warm water

2 Tbsp olive oil

1 Tbsp sugar

1½ tsp salt

2 Tbsp lecithin granules (optional)

1 cup (140g) wholemeal flour

2½ cups (350g) high-grade flour

* Buy or make a mixture of kibbled wheat, red and/or purple wheat, and kibbled rye

Prepare the Kibble
Place the kibble mix in a small pot with 2–3 cups (420g) of cold water. Bring to the boil, then simmer for 1–2 minutes. Take from the heat and drain well in a sieve.

Bread Machine Instructions
Carefully measure all the ingredients, including the prepared kibble combined with the measured water, into a 750g capacity bread machine in the order specified by the manufacturer.

Set to the NORMAL/WHITE bread cycle, MEDIUM crust and START. This is a good timer bread.

Hand-made Bread Instructions
In a large bowl mix the prepared kibbled grains with 1¼ cups warm water. Add all the remaining ingredients except the high-grade flour. Mix thoroughly, cover and leave for 15 minutes in a warm place.

Stir in the high-grade flour, adding a little extra water or flour if necessary, to make a dough just firm enough to knead.

Knead with the dough hook of an electric mixer or by hand on a lightly floured surface for 10 minutes, adding extra flour if necessary, until the dough forms a soft ball that springs back when gently pressed.

Turn dough in 2–3 teaspoons of oil in the cleaned dry bowl, cover with cling film and leave in a warm draught-free place for 30 minutes.

Lightly knead the oiled dough in the bowl for 1 minute. Pat the dough into a square shape a little longer than the baking pan, then roll into a cylinder. Put into the sprayed or buttered bread pan, pressing it into the corners and levelling the top.

Leave to rise in a warm, draught-free place for about 1 hour or until double its original size. If desired, brush with milk or egg glaze (page 87) and sprinkle with extra kibbled grains, then bake at 200°C for about 30 minutes until the sides and bottom are browned and the loaf sounds hollow when tapped underneath.

Heavy Multigrain Bread

To get a flattish loaf like the dense multigrain breads available at bakeries, you need a much wetter than normal bread dough.

Makes 1 large loaf (6–8 cup pan):

¾ cup (125g) mixed kibbled grains*

3 tsp Surebake yeast

1¾ cups warm water

2 tsp sugar

1½ tsp salt

1 Tbsp lecithin granules or butter

3 Tbsp non-fat milk powder

2 Tbsp gluten flour

3 cups (420g) wholemeal flour

* Buy or make a mixture of kibbled wheat, red and/or purple wheat, and kibbled rye.

Prepare the Kibble
Place the kibble mix in a pot and cover with cold water. Bring to the boil, then remove from the heat. Allow to stand for a few minutes, then drain in a sieve.

Bread Machine Instructions
Carefully measure all the ingredients including the prepared kibble along with 1¾ cups warm water into a 750g capacity bread machine in the order specified by the manufacturer.

Try the NORMAL/WHITE bread cycle, MEDIUM crust setting, but you may find that you need to experiment with other settings to get the best results from your machine.

Check the dough after about 5 minutes of mixing — it should barely be holding its round shape. Add extra water or a little more flour if required.

Hand-made Bread Instructions
Prepare the kibble mix according to the instructions above. Put in a large bowl with 1¾ cups warm water and the remaining ingredients and mix thoroughly.

Knead with the dough hook of an electric mixer for about 10 minutes. Spread the wet mixture evenly in a well-sprayed or buttered 6–8 cup loaf pan and leave to rise in a warm draught-free place for 45–60 minutes or until double its original size.

Bake at 180°C for 45–60 minutes or until a skewer inserted deeply in the centre of the loaf comes out clean, and the bread sounds hollow when tapped on the bottom.

NOTE: Whether you are making this loaf in a bread machine or by hand, you may have to adjust the quantities of flour and water a little. (We have found this necessary when changing bags of flour.) The mixture should be pourable and spreadable, with a consistency somewhere between a very soft dough and a batter. Leave for 24 hours before slicing.

Dark Rye Bread

This large loaf has a wonderfully rich dark colour, an inviting aroma, an interesting flavour, and is very popular. You can vary the colour and flavour of the bread to suit your own taste.

Makes 1 large loaf (8 cup capacity tin):

3 tsp Surebake yeast

1½ cups warm water

2 Tbsp golden syrup

2 Tbsp oil

1½ tsp salt

2 cups (280g) high-grade flour

1½ (180g) cups rye meal

2 Tbsp cocoa powder

1 tsp instant coffee granules

about 1 tsp caraway seeds

Bread Machine Instructions

Carefully measure all the ingredients into a 750g capacity bread machine in the order specified by the manufacturer.

Set to the NORMAL/WHITE bread cycle, MEDIUM crust and START (or use DOUGH cycle and shape and bake as below). This is a good timer bread.

Hand-made Bread Instructions

Measure the first five ingredients into a large bowl with 1 cup of high-grade flour and mix thoroughly. Cover and leave to stand in a warm place for 15 minutes.

Stir in the high-grade flour, rye meal, cocoa powder, instant coffee and caraway seeds. Add a little extra flour or water to make a dough just firm enough to knead.

Knead with the dough hook of an electric mixer or by hand on a lightly floured surface for 10 minutes, adding extra flour if necessary, until the dough forms a soft ball that springs back when gently pressed.

Turn in 2–3 teaspoons of oil in the cleaned dry bowl, cover with cling film and leave in a warm draught-free place for 30 minutes.

Lightly knead the dough in the bowl for 1 minute before turning out onto a lightly floured surface.

To make a round loaf pat the dough into a ball, flatten it slightly with your hand, then pick it up and tuck and pinch all the edges underneath, so the top of the dough is smooth and stretched, forming an evenly rounded loaf when baked.

To help keep its shape, put the round loaf in a 23cm round pan (preferably loose-bottomed) and dust with flour. Leave in a warm draught-free place for about 1 hour or until risen to about twice its original size.

Bake at 200°C for about 30 minutes or until the loaf sounds hollow when the bottom is tapped.

VARIATION: For a light rye loaf, leave out the cocoa powder and instant coffee. Vary the amount of caraway seed to suit your taste.

Herbed Parmesan Bread

Serve this herby bread with soup or salad to make a substantial light meal or try brushing thick slices with garlic oil and grilling them for an interesting snack.

Makes 1 large loaf (8 cup pan):

3 tsp Surebake yeast

1¼ cups warm water

2 Tbsp lecithin granules or oil

2 tsp sugar

1 tsp salt

1 cup (140g) wholemeal flour

2 cups (280g) high-grade flour

¼ cup grated Parmesan cheese

¼ cup basil pesto

¼ cup finely chopped fresh herbs

Bread Machine Instructions

Carefully measure all the ingredients into a 750g capacity bread machine in the order specified by the manufacturer.

Set to the NORMAL/WHITE bread cycle, MEDIUM crust and START (or use the DOUGH cycle and shape and bake as described below). This is a good timer bread.

Hand-made Bread Instructions

Measure the first six ingredients into a large bowl and mix thoroughly. Cover and leave for 15 minutes or longer in a warm place.

Stir in the high-grade flour, grated cheese, pesto and chopped herbs, then stir to make a soft dough just firm enough to knead, adding a little extra flour if necessary.

Knead with the dough hook of an electric mixer or by hand on a lightly floured surface for 10 minutes, adding extra flour if necessary, until the dough forms a soft ball that springs back when gently pressed.

Turn the dough in 2–3 teaspoons of oil in the cleaned dry bowl, cover with cling film and leave in a warm draught-free place for about 30 minutes.

Lightly knead the oiled dough in the bowl for 1 minute. Pat the dough into a square shape a little longer than the baking pan, then roll into a cylinder. Put into the sprayed or buttered bread pan, pressing it into the corners and levelling the top.

Leave to rise in a warm draught-free place for about 1 hour or until the dough has doubled in size.

Brush with milk or egg glaze (page 87) and bake at 200°C for 30 minutes or until the bottom and sides are browned and the loaf sounds hollow when tapped.

VARIATIONS: Use dough to make Monkey bread (page 12) or rolls (page 21).

Sun-dried Tomato Bread

The tomato paste in this bread gives it a warm, sunny colour and the sun-dried tomatoes add a definite tomato flavour. Serve with a light pasta dish and/or salad to make a delicious summer meal.

Makes 1 large loaf (6–8 cup pan):

3 tsp Surebake yeast

1 cup warm water

¼ cup tomato paste

2 tsp sugar

1 tsp salt

2 Tbsp lecithin granules or oil

1 cup (140g) wholemeal flour

2 cups (280g) high-grade flour

¼ cup chopped sun-dried tomatoes

1 Tbsp chopped fresh basil (optional)

Bread Machine Instructions

Carefully measure all the ingredients into a 750g capacity bread machine in the order specified by the manufacturer.

Set to the NORMAL/WHITE bread cycle, MEDIUM crust and START (or use the DOUGH cycle and shape by hand). This is a good timer bread.

Hand-made Bread Instructions

Measure the first seven ingredients into a large bowl and mix thoroughly. Cover and leave for 15 minutes or longer in a warm place.

Stir in the high-grade flour, sun-dried tomatoes, and the basil if using, adding extra high-grade flour if necessary to make a soft dough just firm enough to knead.

Knead with the dough hook of an electric mixer or by hand on a lightly floured surface for 10 minutes until the dough forms a soft ball that springs back when gently pressed.

Turn the dough in 2–3 teaspoons of oil in a cleaned, dry bowl, cover with cling film and leave in a warm draught-free place for about 30 minutes.

Lightly knead the oiled dough in the bowl for 1 minute. Turn it out onto a lightly floured surface, then pat it into a square shape a little longer than the baking pan. Roll the dough into a cylinder, then put into the buttered or sprayed bread pan, pressing it into the corners and levelling the top.

Leave to rise in a warm draught-free place for about 1 hour or until the dough has doubled in size.

If desired, brush with milk or egg glaze (page 87) and bake at 200°C for about 30 minutes or until the loaf has browned on its bottom and sides and sounds hollow when tapped.

VARIATIONS: Spread some basil pesto over the dough before you roll it up or shape the dough as for focaccia (page 31) adding basil pesto and Parmesan cheese (or other) toppings.

Yoghurt Bread or Rolls

These chewy little rolls have a fine texture and an interesting, slightly sour flavour.
They make good dinner rolls and freeze well, too.

Makes 1 large loaf or 12 rolls:

3 tsp Surebake yeast

¾ cup plain unsweetened yoghurt

½ cup warm water

2 Tbsp lecithin granules or oil

2 tsp sugar

1 tsp salt

3 cups (420g) high-grade flour

Bread Machine Instructions

Carefully measure all the ingredients into a 750g capacity bread machine in the order specified by the manufacturer. Set to the NORMAL/WHITE bread cycle, MEDIUM crust and START (or use the DOUGH cycle and shape and bake as described below). This is a good timer bread.

NOTE: The thickness of yoghurt varies, so check the dough after about 5 minutes of mixing in your bread machine and add a little extra water if it looks too dry.

Hand-made Bread Instructions

Measure the first six ingredients into a large bowl with 1 cup of the flour and mix thoroughly. Cover and leave for 15 minutes or longer in a warm place. Add the rest of the flour and stir to make a soft dough, adding a little extra warm water or flour if necessary.

Knead with the dough hook of an electric mixer or by hand on a lightly floured surface for 10 minutes, adding extra water or flour if necessary, until the dough is smooth and satiny and springs back when gently pressed.

Turn the dough in 1–2 teaspoons of oil in the cleaned dry bowl, cover with cling film and leave in a warm draught-free place for 30 minutes. Lightly knead the oiled dough in the bowl for 1 minute.

Shaping and Baking

Roll the dough into a single long loaf or cut into 12 equal pieces (each about 75g). Roll each piece into a 12cm-long sausage shape or into round rolls. (For smooth-topped round rolls, make your thumb and forefinger in a ring shape and push a piece of dough through the formed ring, so the dough on the top of the roll is stretched and the edges are pinched together underneath.)

If making a long loaf, place it diagonally on an oiled oven tray. In the case of rolls, place them on two oiled oven trays, leaving room between them to spread.

Leave to rise in a warm draught-free place for about 1 hour or until doubled in size/thickness. After 30 minutes diagonally slash the top/s of the rolls or loaf using a very sharp knife.

Brush with milk or egg glaze (page 87), then bake at 200°C until the top/s and bottom/s are evenly browned, about 15 minutes for the rolls or 20–25 minutes for a single long loaf.

Hamburger and Hot Dog Buns

These tasty white buns and rolls are just right for home-made hot dogs and hamburgers.

For about 8 buns or rolls:

3 tsp Surebake yeast

1 cup warm water

50g butter

1 Tbsp sugar

1 tsp salt

2 Tbsp non-fat milk powder

3 cups (420g) high-grade flour

toasted sesame seeds (optional)

Bread Machine Instructions

Carefully measure all the ingredients into a 750g capacity bread machine, in the order specified by the manufacturer. Set to the DOUGH cycle, and START. When the cycle is complete, remove the dough from the machine and shape, then bake as below.

Hand-made Bread Instructions

Measure the first six ingredients into a large bowl with 1½ cups of the flour and mix thoroughly. Cover and leave for 15 minutes or longer in a warm place.

Stir in the remaining flour, adding as much as you need to make a dough just firm enough to knead.

Knead with the dough hook of an electric mixer or by hand on a lightly floured surface for 10 minutes, adding extra flour if necessary.

Turn in 2–3 teaspoons of oil in the cleaned dry bowl, cover with cling film and leave in a warm draught-free place for 30–40 minutes.

Lightly knead the dough in the bowl for 1 minute, then turn out onto a lightly floured surface.

Shaping and Baking

Divide dough into eight pieces, each about 100g. For hamburger buns: roll each piece into a smooth ball, then flatten into 9cm rounds. For hot dog buns: roll each piece of dough into a cigar shape about 18cm long.

Arrange on oiled or well-sprayed baking trays and leave to rise in a warm draught-free place for about 1 hour or until the buns have approximately doubled in size.

Brush with egg glaze (page 87) and sprinkle with toasted sesame seeds if desired. Bake at 200°C for 12–15 minutes until golden brown top and bottom.

Pizzas and Pita Breads

One of the real joys of owning a bread machine is discovering how easy it is to make good yeasty pizza bases. Simply measure in the ingredients, set to the dough cycle and go away. The hardest part becomes selecting your toppings!

Makes 1 very large pizza, 2 medium pizzas or 8 medium pita breads:

2 tsp active dried yeast

1 cup warm water plus 2 Tbsp

2 tsp sugar

1 tsp salt

2 Tbsp olive oil

3 cups (420g) high-grade flour

Bread Machine Instructions

Carefully measure all the ingredients into a 750g capacity bread machine in the order specified by the manufacturer.

Set to DOUGH cycle and START. When the cycle is complete, take the dough out of the machine and shape and bake as below.

Hand-made Bread Instructions

Measure the first five ingredients into a large bowl with 1 cup of the measured flour and mix thoroughly. Cover and leave for 15 minutes or longer in a warm place. Stir in the remaining flour, adding extra if necessary, to make a dough just firm enough to knead.

Knead with the dough hook of an electric mixer or by hand on a lightly floured surface for 10 minutes, adding extra flour if necessary, until the dough forms a soft ball that springs back when gently pressed.

Turn the dough in 2–3 teaspoons of oil in the cleaned dry bowl, cover with cling film and leave in a warm draught-free place for about 30 minutes. Lightly knead the risen dough, then shape.

To shape and bake pizzas: roll dough into thin circles, according to the number and size of pizzas you require. Place on sprayed pizza pans, Teflon liners, baking paper, or well-oiled baking sheets.

Add your favourite toppings (see below) and bake at 225°C until the underside is brown. For crisp, very thin pizza bake before (and after) adding desired topping.

To shape and bake pita breads: cut the dough into eight equal pieces, then on a well-floured board roll out each piece into a 15–18cm circle, sprinkling with extra flour as needed. Leave to stand for at least 10 minutes.

Place a baking sheet on a rack in the middle of the oven. Heat the oven to its highest temperature. Ideally, place a cast-iron pan or griddle on the rack below the middle one (it will heat up and compensate for heat loss when the oven door is opened).

Slide a shaped pita bread onto a piece of floured (to prevent sticking) cardboard, then, opening the oven door for as brief a time as possible, slide the bread onto the hot baking sheet. In 1–2 minutes the bread should puff up dramatically, then collapse a little.

Lift out the cooked bread with tongs after 2–3 minutes and put in the next one to cook. Pile the hot breads in a plastic bag so they do not dry out.

Pizza Topping Suggestions

- Tomato paste, sun-dried tomato paste, dried tomato pesto, sliced tomatoes, drained canned seasoned tomatoes

- Red, yellow and green peppers, roasted red and orange pepper strips and eggplant

- Onion slices, caramelised onions, chopped spring onions, roasted garlic

- Sliced mushrooms, sliced/whole olives, fresh and dried herbs, artichoke hearts

- Anchovy fillets, salmon and shrimps, salami, ham, bacon, turkey and chicken

- Mozzarella, grated tasty cheese, camembert and brie, Parmesan, feta

Breadsticks and Broccoli Cheese Bread

Pizza dough is easy to make and work with. Use it when you feel like experimenting! We find it to be excellent for breadsticks, as well as for unusual savoury rolls filled with vegetables and cheese.

Filling:

1 onion, chopped

¼ cup olive oil

500g broccoli

¼ tsp oregano

2–3 Tbsp water

½ tsp salt

freshly ground black pepper

2 cups grated tasty or Parmesan cheese plus extra for sprinkling

Broccoli Cheese Bread

Although the idea of a vegetable-filled bread may seem rather odd, this is one of our favourite breads — its bright green filling is both attractive and unusual.

Make the pizza dough on page 22 in a bread machine or by hand. Prepare the filling while the dough rises.

In a medium pot cook the onion in the oil until transparent, but not browned. Cut or break the broccoli into small almond-sized florets. Peel and chop all the stems into pieces the same size. Add to the onion with the oregano and water. Cover and cook over high heat for 2–3 minutes until the broccoli is barely tender and the water has evaporated. Add the seasonings and cool.

After the dough has risen for the last time, roll it out on a floured board until it measures about 40x40cm. Arrange the cooled broccoli over the dough, leaving 2cm clear along one side. Dampen the uncovered strip with cold water. Cover the broccoli with the grated cheese and roll up (like a sponge roll), uncovered side last.

Cut the roll into 16 even pieces. Place cut-side up, in a buttered or oiled 23cm square cake pan. Cover and leave to rise in a warm draught-free place for about 30 minutes or until double original size.

Sprinkle with extra grated cheese and bake at 200°C for 30 minutes or until nicely browned. Serve warm.

Breadsticks

Make the pizza dough recipe on page 22 in a bread machine or by hand.

Roll the dough into a 25x30cm rectangle. Preferably using a cleaver or a heavy long-bladed knife, cut it into 25 strips, each 1cm wide and 30cm long.

Arrange on baking paper or a Teflon liner, on one or more oven trays, about 1cm apart. After you have cut and placed the last strip, brush with egg glaze (page 87), sprinkle with Parmesan cheese, poppy or sesame seeds and bake at 150°C for 30–40 minutes until they are evenly golden brown and crisp right through. (Start checking after 20 minutes, since ovens vary a great deal.)

Bake breadsticks until they are completely dry, then pack them in airtight containers and store them until ready to use (e.g. to serve with soup).

Calzone and Stromboli

Try making these fashionable foods using pizza dough in different ways and enclosing whatever fillings you like. The results are sure to be popular with all age groups.

Calzone

Calzone is a pizza folded in half and sealed before it is baked.

Make the pizza dough recipe on page 22 in a bread machine or by hand. After the dough has risen for the last time, cut into eight even pieces. Roll each piece into a 20cm circle, adding enough flour to stop it sticking to the rolling pin and work surface.

Cover half of each circle with your choice of pizza toppings or the filling for the Broccoli Cheese Bread (page 24), leaving an uncovered rim of about 1.5cm. Moisten the rim with water, then fold the uncovered half over the topping and seal the edges.
Lift onto a baking sheet, cut several air vents in the dough, then leave to rise for about 10 minutes.

Bake at 220°C for about 10 minutes. Serve warm.

Stromboli

This wonderfully tasty and portable strudel-like treat is made from thin layers of pizza dough and your favourite fillings.

Make the pizza dough on page 22 in a bread machine or by hand. After the dough has risen for the last time, cut the dough into two equal pieces. Working on a well-floured bench, roll the dough very thinly into a 40x50cm rectangle, making sure the dough does not stick.

Filling A: ¼ cup each diced ham, diced salami, grated tasty cheese and Parmesan cheese

Filling B: 2–3 Tbsp basil pesto, ¼ cup each sun-dried tomato paste, diced salami, diced ham and 1 cup grated tasty cheese

Spread the ingredients for the filling of your choice over the dough, then roll up as you would a sponge roll.

Carefully lift the filled roll onto a baking sheet lined with baking paper or a Teflon liner and position so the join is underneath.

Bake at 200°C for about 12 minutes or until golden brown. Serve warm or cold, cut in diagonal slices.

Sourdough Starter

2 cups high-grade flour

1 cup low-fat milk or unsweetened yoghurt

1 cup water

1 tsp active dried yeast

These days we tend to buy the yeast we need without a second thought, but not so long ago the only yeast available to people in isolated places was a home-made culture or "starter", in the form of a flour and water mixture in which wild yeasts were grown. The yeasts in the starter mixture were left to grow and multiply in a jar or crock, which was kept in a cool place in summer and a warm place in winter.

As some of this starter was used to rise bread, more flour and water was added to feed the remaining yeasts. Good starters (which made well-risen breads with a good flavour and texture) were treasured by their owners, used for many years, and passed on to friends and relations.

On standing, a starter turns sour, and gives bread made from it an interesting tangy flavour, much sought after today in places such as San Francisco.

The sourdough starter we make today is more refined than those early starters, which utilised wild yeasts that floated around in the kitchen. Our recipe starts with a little bread yeast that grows in a flour mixture in a very clean, carefully covered container.

The resulting starter works well, producing bread with an interesting sour flavour. Should we use up the starter, or let it die and make another starter, chances are it will taste slightly different – it may be even better or it may not!

To prepare a simple starter, mix the ingredients in a clean jar, leaving about ¼ of the jar clear for headspace.

Cover the jar and leave it in a warm room, out of the sun, for 4–7 days, depending on the temperature. Each day, stir the starter with a clean spoon.

For the first few days it may have a tendency to bubble up and overflow, but it will quieten down and become thinner after a few days. Refrigerate in a lidded jar after the mixture takes on a definite sour smell and develops a clear layer on top.

Keep it free from contamination. A slight greyish colour is fine, but if it develops a nasty smell or changes colour, especially pink or purple, throw it out and start again.

To use the starter, stir well and pour off as much as you need. Replace each cup used with a cup of water mixed with a cup of high-grade flour. Leave the jar at room temperature for a day before using any more of its contents or refrigerating it again.

If you do not use your starter regularly, throw out or give away a cupful of it once a week and add fresh flour and water as above.

Bread made with only a starter needs a long rising time. Extra yeast is often used to speed up the process, and the starter is used for the characteristic flavour it provides.

If you are nervous about starting your own culture (starter) you can actually buy one instead – this can be quite fun as sometimes the culture can be traced back for decades.

We haven't been able to find a local supplier yet, but Sourdoughs International (www.sourdo.com) and King Arthur Flour (www.kingarthurflour.com) are both US-based companies that will supply cultures internationally. (Note: When you fill in the King Arthur online order form, it may not appear that they will ship outside of the USA, but if you send them a message it can be arranged.)

Sourdough Focaccia

In days gone by, doughs were risen by adding a little dough reserved from the previous day, or by adding "sourdough" starter giving a distinctive sourdough flavour.

Makes 2 flat loaves each about 20x30cm:

1 cup sourdough starter (page 27)

1 cup warm water

1 Tbsp sugar

1 tsp salt

1 tsp active dried yeast

3 cups (420g) high-grade flour

1–2 Tbsp olive oil

sliced black olives

coarse rock or flaky salt

pesto

fresh rosemary

Parmesan cheese, etc

Bread Machine Instructions

Carefully measure the first six ingredients into a 750g capacity bread machine in the order specified by the manufacturer. Set to the DOUGH cycle and START. When the dough cycle is complete, shape and bake as below.

Hand-made Bread Instructions

Measure sourdough starter, warm water, sugar and salt together into a large bowl, sprinkle over the yeast and leave to stand for 5 minutes. Add half the high-grade flour, mix thoroughly, cover then leave to stand for 15 minutes or longer in a warm place.

Stir in the remaining flour, adding a little extra warm water or high-grade flour if necessary, to make a dough just firm enough to knead.

Knead with the dough hook of an electric mixer or by hand on a lightly floured surface for 10 minutes, adding extra flour if necessary.

Turn the dough in 2–3 teaspoons of oil in the cleaned dry bowl. Cover with cling film and leave to stand for at least 1 hour. (The longer the dough stands, the better the flavour. It will keep in the refrigerator for 12–18 hours.) After standing, lightly knead for about 1 minute.

Shaping and Baking

Divide the dough in half and roll each piece into a rectangle about 20x30cm. Gently press each piece into an olive-oiled rectangular baking pan about the same size as the rolled-out dough, then use your index finger to make small depressions all over the surface.

Spread with one or more of the listed toppings, letting some of the mixture fill the holes. Sprinkle with Parmesan cheese or coarse (rock) salt.

Leave to rise in a warm, draught-free place for 30–60 minutes, then drizzle with a little more olive oil and bake at 220°C for 10–15 minutes or until golden brown top and bottom. Serve warm, cut in fingers or rectangles, soon after cooking.

NOTE: Don't forget to replenish your starter by adding another cup of flour and a cup of water.

Sourdough Loaf

If you like the tang and texture of sourdough breads, this recipe is for you!

Makes 1 large loaf or 16 rolls:

1½ cups sourdough starter (page 27)

½ cup milk

1 Tbsp oil

1 Tbsp sugar

1 tsp salt

3½ cups (490g) high-grade flour

2 tsp Surebake yeast

NOTE: You can control the degree of sourness by increasing or decreasing the length of time that the sourdough mixture sits at room temperature before baking.

Bread Machine Instructions

Measure all ingredients into the bread machine in the order specified by the manufacturer and start the machine. Use the NORMAL/WHITE bread cycle, and MEDIUM crust settings (or use the DOUGH cycle and shape and bake by hand).

Hand-made Bread Instructions

Combine the first five ingredients in a large bowl with half the flour. Add the yeast and mix thoroughly. Cover and leave for 15 minutes or longer in a warm place.

Add the rest of the flour and stir to make a soft dough, adding a little extra warm water or flour if necessary, just firm enough to knead.

Knead with the dough hook of an electric mixer or by hand on a lightly floured surface for 10 minutes.

Turn the dough in 2–3 teaspoons of oil in the cleaned dry bowl, cover with cling film and leave in a warm draught-free place for 30 minutes. Lightly knead the dough, and then shape as desired.

Shaping and Baking

Roll the dough into one large round ball and put in a 20–25cm cake pan or divide evenly into 16 pieces and shape each into a small round roll.

Leave to rise in a warm draught-free place for 40 minutes, slash tops with a very sharp blade if desired, then leave for 20 minutes longer or until double original size.

Bake at 210°C, 10–12 minutes for rolls or about 30 minutes for a large loaf, until bread is evenly brown, top and bottom. For a hard crust, mist with a water spray before and during the first few minutes of cooking or put a roasting dish containing 1cm boiling water in the bottom of the oven 1 minute before you put the bread in.

NOTE: Don't forget to replenish or feed your starter by adding 1½ cups of flour and 1½ cups of water.

Focaccia

We're not sure exactly what it is about these Italian-style flat breads that makes them so appealing, but this is another of our favourites. Try it plain, or with some of our favourite toppings, but really these are only a start...

Makes 1 loaf about 22x32cm:

2 tsp Surebake yeast

1½ cups water

1 Tbsp sugar

1 tsp salt

1 Tbsp olive oil

3 cups (420g) high-grade flour

1 tsp dried oregano

1 Tbsp olive oil

coarse rock or flaky salt

Bread Machine Instructions

Carefully measure the first seven ingredients into a 750g capacity bread machine in the order specified by the manufacturer.

Set to the DOUGH cycle and START. When the cycle is complete shape and bake as below.

Hand-made Bread Instructions

Measure the first five ingredients into a large bowl with 1½ cups of the high-grade flour and mix thoroughly. Cover and leave for 15 minutes or longer in a warm place.

Stir in the remaining flour and the oregano, adding a little extra warm water or bread flour if necessary to make a dough just firm enough to knead.

Knead with the dough hook of an electric mixer or by hand on a lightly floured surface for 10 minutes, adding extra flour if necessary, until the dough forms a soft dough that springs back when gently pressed.

Turn the dough in 2–3 teaspoons of oil in the cleaned dry bowl, cover with cling film and leave in a warm draught-free place for about 30 minutes.

Lightly knead the oiled dough in the bowl for about 1 minute.

Shaping and Baking

Turn the dough out onto a lightly floured board and roll into a 20x30cm rectangle. Place on a well-oiled baking sheet or in a sponge roll tin and leave to rise in a warm, draught-free place for about 1 hour or until double its original size.

Pour the second measure of oil evenly over the surface, then using your index finger poke the dough to create a series of indentations. Sprinkle with flaky or rock salt or any of the following toppings:

- 2 tablespoons each pesto and olive oil mixed to a paste with ¼ cup grated Parmesan cheese
- coarsely chopped sun-dried tomatoes
- anchovies
- sliced or whole black olives

Bake at 225°C for 15 minutes or until golden brown top and bottom.

Simon's All-purpose Bread

This is Simon's "go to" bread recipe – made so often he has it committed to memory. The dough works well as a pizza base, makes a good loaf if left to bake in his bread machine, or can be run through the dough cycle, then shaped into a focaccia-style or Vienna loaf that always seems to get plenty of compliments. The flavour of the bread is particularly good when the dough is made well ahead, then left to rest for several hours (or even overnight) before being shaped then risen again before baking.

For 1 large Vienna or focaccia-type loaf or 2 large pizzas:

¾ cup milk

½ cup hot water

2 tsp active dried yeast

½ tsp Surebake yeast

2 tsp sugar

1½ tsp salt

2 Tbsp olive oil

3 cups (420g) high-grade flour

Bread Machine Instructions

Carefully measure all the ingredients into a 750g capacity bread machine in the order specified by the manufacturer.

Set to the NORMAL/WHITE bread cycle, MEDIUM crust and START or use the DOUGH cycle and shape and bake by hand. You can leave the dough to sit (in the machine if the weather is cooler, or in an oiled bowl in the fridge in warmer weather) for several hours at this stage.

Hand-made Bread Instructions

Measure the first seven ingredients into a large bowl with 1½ cups of the flour and mix thoroughly. Cover and leave for 15 minutes or longer in a warm place.

Stir in the remaining flour, adding a little extra warm water or bread flour if necessary to make a dough just firm enough to knead.

Knead with the dough hook of an electric mixer or by hand on a lightly floured surface for 10 minutes, adding extra flour if necessary, until the dough forms a soft dough that springs back when gently pressed.

Shaping and Baking

To make pizzas, divide the dough in two and shape and bake as described on page 22.

Otherwise turn the dough in 2–3 teaspoons of oil in the cleaned dry bowl, cover with cling film and leave to sit for at least 30 minutes (you can leave it for several hours at this stage – on the bench if the weather is cooler or in the fridge in warmer weather).

When you are ready to proceed, lightly knead the oiled dough in the bowl for about 1 minute.

Turn out the dough onto a lightly floured board and roll into a 30x20cm oval shape. For a Vienna-type loaf roll it up into a sausage shape and place on a well-oiled baking sheet or in a sponge roll tin and leave to rise in a warm, draught-free place for about 1 hour or until double its original size.

For a focaccia-style loaf place the dough on a well-oiled baking sheet and pat it out to about 2cm thick. Leave to rise in a warm, draught-free place for about 1 hour or until roughly double its original size. Drizzle with a little extra oil, then using your index finger poke the dough at intervals over the surface. Sprinkle with flaky or rock salt or any of the toppings suggested on page 31.

Bake at 225°C for 15 minutes or until golden brown top and bottom.

Garlic and Olive Bread

Even if you do not like olives we think you will enjoy the savoury, but not overpowering flavour of this soft, crusty bread. Serve with Mediterranean food, enjoy it by itself, or use it to make the most delicious crostini.

Makes 1 large round or brick-shaped loaf (6–8 cup pan):

3 tsp Surebake yeast

1¼ cups warm water

2 Tbsp olive oil

2 tsp sugar

1 tsp salt

¼ cup non-fat dried milk powder

3 cups (420g) high-grade flour

¼ cup grated Parmesan cheese

2 cloves garlic, chopped

1 Tbsp chopped fresh basil

1 tsp chopped fresh thyme leaves

¼ cup chopped black olives

Bread Machine Instructions

Carefully measure all the ingredients into a 750g capacity bread machine in the order specified by the manufacturer. Set to the NORMAL/WHITE bread cycle, MEDIUM crust and START. This is a good timer bread.

Hand-made Bread Instructions

Measure the first six ingredients into a large bowl. Add 1½ cups of the flour and mix thoroughly. Cover and leave for 15 minutes or longer in a warm place.

Stir in the rest of the flour along with the remaining ingredients, adding a little warm water or flour if necessary, to make a dough just firm enough to knead.

Knead with the dough hook of an electric mixer or by hand on a lightly floured surface for 10 minutes, adding extra flour if necessary, until the dough forms a soft ball that springs back when gently pressed.

Turn the dough in 1–2 teaspoons of oil in the cleaned dry bowl, then cover with cling film and leave in a warm draught-free place for about 30 minutes.

Lightly knead the oiled dough in the bowl for about 1 minute, then turn out onto a lightly floured surface.

Shaping and Baking

To make a round loaf, shape into a ball and flatten slightly onto a lightly-oiled baking sheet. For a regular loaf, pat or roll the dough into a square a little larger than the pan, then roll up into a cylinder. Place the shaped dough into the buttered or sprayed pan.

Leave to rise in a warm draught-free place for about 1 hour or until double its original size.

Brush with milk or egg glaze (page 87) if desired, then bake at 200°C for about 35 minutes until the sides and bottom of the loaf are brown and it sounds hollow when tapped underneath.

To make crostini, cut the baked bread into 5mm slices, place on baking sheets and brush lightly with olive oil. Bake at 150°C for about 7 minutes or until golden brown and crisp. Cool before storing in an airtight container.

Ciabatta

This is one of several authentic Italian recipes translated for us by some very generous volunteers. Using a traditional approach, this crusty bread is made in two stages, i.e. started and then left to ferment overnight, then completed and baked the next day.
We love it when we get loaves that have a really open (holey) texture, but it may take a little practice to get your ciabatta exactly the way you want it. In any case the long fermentation will give it a very good flavour.

Makes 1 large flat loaf:

1 tsp active dried yeast

1½ cups warm water

2½ cups (350g) high-grade flour

2 Tbsp gluten flour

2 tsp active dried yeast

½ cup warm water

2 tsp malt

1½ tsp salt

1 cup (140g) high-grade flour

Bread Machine Instructions

Carefully measure the first four ingredients into a 750g capacity bread machine in the order specified by the manufacturer. Set to the DOUGH cycle and START. When the cycle is complete place the dough in a large bowl, cover and leave to rise at room temperature for at least 12 hours. .

After rising, put the dough back into the bread machine with the remaining five ingredients. Set to the DOUGH cycle and START. Check after 2 minutes mixing – the dough should be very wet, barely forming a ball while the paddle is turning. When it stops the dough should flow to the edges of the bowl. If too firm, add water a little at a time until it is wet enough. When the cycle is complete, shape and bake as below.

Hand-made Bread Instructions

In a large bowl sprinkle the first measure of yeast over the warm water and leave to stand for several minutes before adding the first quantity of flour and the gluten. Mix thoroughly, cover with cling film and leave to rise at room temperature for at least 12 hours.

In the large bowl of an electric mixer fitted with a dough hook, combine the remaining ingredients with the risen dough mixture and knead well. The dough should be too soft to knead by hand, flowing to the edges of the bowl when you turn off the mixer. Add extra warm water if necessary. Knead for 10 minutes. Remove the dough hook, cover the bowl with cling film and leave in a warm draught-free place for 30–40 minutes.

Shaping and Baking

Gently tip the very soft dough onto a well-floured baking sheet covered with baking paper or a Teflon liner, taking care not to knock the air from the dough. Sprinkle generously with flour and shape into a 35x20cm oblong. Leave to rise in a warm draught-free place for 40–50 minutes.

Heat the oven to 240°C. To ensure a good crust put 1cm of hot water in a roasting dish in the bottom of the oven 5 minutes before you put in the bread. Bake for 20–25 minutes (removing the dish of water after 10 minutes) until the loaf is crusty and evenly browned top and bottom, and sounds hollow when tapped. Leave the cooked bread to cool for 5–10 minutes in the switched-off oven with the door open.

French Bread

It is hard to believe that such a basic dough can produce such delicious crusty French bread. Leaving the dough to stand overnight requires a little patience and some forethought, but in the end it's worth the wait.

Makes 1 large or 2 smaller baguettes:

2 tsp active dried yeast

1¼ cups warm water

2 tsp sugar

1½ tsp salt

3 cups (420g) high-grade flour

Bread Machine Instructions

Carefully measure all the ingredients into a 750g capacity bread machine in the order specified by the manufacturer.

Set to the DOUGH cycle and START. When the cycle is complete, allow to stand as described below before kneading, etc.

Hand-made Bread Instructions

Measure the first four ingredients into a large bowl with 1½ cups of the flour and mix thoroughly. Cover and leave for 15 minutes in a warm place.

Stir in the remaining flour, and a little extra flour or water if necessary, to make a dough just firm enough to knead.

Knead with the dough hook of an electric mixer or by hand on a lightly floured board for 10 minutes until the dough forms a soft ball that springs back when gently pressed.

Rising, Shaping and Baking

Turn the dough in 2–3 teaspoons of oil in the cleaned dry bowl. Cover with cling film and leave for at least 2 hours or preferably overnight at room temperature. It may be necessary to punch (or press) down the dough several times during this period.

Very lightly knead the dough in the bowl (just for a few seconds), then turn out onto a lightly floured board. Roll and shape the dough into one long characteristic French loaf (or divide the dough in half to make two smaller loaves).

Leave to rise at room temperature for about 1–1½ hours or until about doubled in size. Using a very sharp knife make a series of 4–5 diagonal slashes about 5mm deep on the top of the loaf or loaves.

Heat the oven to 220°C. At least 5 minutes before the bread is due to go into the oven put a roasting dish with 1cm of hot water in the bottom of the oven. To get a really chewy crust, spray the loaf with a fine mist of water before it goes in the oven, then spray again after 2 minutes.

Bake for 15 minutes, removing the dish of water from the oven after 10 minutes. The loaf or loaves should be golden brown and sound hollow when tapped. Eat within 12 hours of baking.

NOTE: For a loaf with a more open texture, add 2 tablespoons gluten with the flour. Add extra water as necessary; you'll probably need about ¼ cup.

Cottage Cheese Bread

This nearly white loaf keeps well, staying fresh for two or three days. Nobody will guess what it is that makes the loaf so moist and delicious!

Makes a 20cm "cottage" loaf:

3 tsp Surebake yeast

½ cup cottage cheese

1 large egg

¾ cup warm water

2 Tbsp lecithin granules or oil

1 Tbsp sugar

1½ tsp salt

2½ cups (350g) high-grade flour

½ cup (70g) wholemeal flour

2 Tbsp non-fat milk powder (optional)

Bread Machine Instructions

Carefully measure all the ingredients into a 750g capacity bread machine in the order specified by the manufacturer.

Set to the NORMAL/WHITE bread cycle, MEDIUM crust and START (or use the DOUGH cycle and shape and bake by hand as described below).

Hand-made Bread Instructions

Measure the first seven ingredients into a large bowl. Add 1½ cups of the measured high-grade flour and the milk powder, if using, and mix thoroughly. Cover and leave for 15 minutes or longer in a warm place.

Stir in the remaining flour, adding a little extra warm water or high-grade flour if necessary, to make a dough just firm enough to knead.

Knead with the dough hook of an electric mixer or by hand on a lightly floured surface for 10 minutes, adding extra flour if necessary, until the dough forms a soft ball that springs back when gently pressed.

Turn the dough in a little oil in the cleaned dry bowl, cover, and leave in a warm draught-free place for about 30 minutes.

Lightly knead the oiled dough in the bowl for 1 minute, then turn out onto a lightly floured surface.

Shaping and Baking

Shape three-quarters of the dough into a ball, then flatten with the palm of your hand until it is about 15cm in diameter. Roll the remaining dough into a smaller ball, about 9cm. Lightly dampen the surface of the larger ball with a little water, then place the smaller ball on top. Press your index finger through the small ball through to the centre of the large one, creating a hole through the centre of the small ball.

Leave to rise in a warm draught-free place for about 1 hour or until double its original size.

For a crisp crust, spray with a fine mist of water or for a thin glazed crust brush with milk or an egg glaze (page 87) and bake at 200°C for 15–30 minutes until evenly golden brown and hollow sounding when tapped. Longer cooking will make a thicker crust.

High Protein Bread

This nicely flavoured bread, derived from a recipe developed by Cornell University, has several added high protein ingredients, and produces a large, extra-nutritious loaf.

Makes 1 large loaf (6–8 cup pan):

3 tsp Surebake yeast

1½ cups warm water

2 Tbsp lecithin granules or oil

2 Tbsp honey

1½ tsp salt

½ cup non-fat milk powder

2 cups (280g) high-grade flour

1 Tbsp gluten flour (optional)

1½ cups (210g) wholemeal flour

½ cup each soya flour and wheat germ

Bread Machine Instructions

Carefully measure all the ingredients into a 750g capacity bread machine in the order specified by the manufacturer. (If using gluten flour, add an extra 2 tablespoons of water.)

Set to the NORMAL/WHITE bread cycle, MEDIUM crust and START (or use the DOUGH cycle and shape and bake by hand). This is a good timer bread.

Hand-made Bread Instructions

Measure the first seven ingredients, plus the gluten flour if using (see note above about extra water), into a large bowl and mix thoroughly. Cover and leave for 15 minutes in a warm place.

Add the remaining ingredients, with a little extra flour or warm water if necessary, to make a dough just firm enough to knead.

Knead with the dough hook of an electric mixer or by hand on a lightly floured surface for 10 minutes, adding extra flour if necessary, until the dough forms a soft ball that springs back when gently pressed.

Turn in 2–3 teaspoons of oil in the cleaned dry bowl, cover with cling film and leave in a warm draught-free place for about 30 minutes.

Lightly knead the oiled dough in the bowl for 1 minute, then turn out onto a lightly floured surface and roll or pat out into a square a little larger than the baking pan. Roll into a cylinder, then put into the buttered or sprayed pan, pressing it into the corners and smoothing the top. (Alternatively, shape into a braid, a large round loaf or rolls, page 88.)

Leave to stand in a warm draught-free place for about 1 hour or until double in size.

Bake at 200°C for 30–40 minutes or until the sides and bottom crust have browned and the loaf sounds hollow when tapped.

Beer Braid

Try making this bread with different beers. Lager will produce a light coloured loaf with a subtle flavour, while darker beers will produce darker bread with stronger flavour. Flat beer works in this recipe, too.

3 tsp Surebake yeast

350ml* beer or lager

1 Tbsp sugar

1 tsp salt

2 Tbsp lecithin granules or oil

1 cup (140g) wholemeal flour

2 cups (280g) high-grade flour

*350ml equals 1½ cups less 5 tsp

Bread Machine Instructions

Carefully measure all the ingredients into a 750g capacity bread machine in the order specified by the manufacturer.

Set to the NORMAL/WHITE cycle, MEDIUM crust and START (or use DOUGH cycle and shape by hand as described below). This is a good timer bread.

Hand-made Bread Instructions

Measure the first six ingredients into a large bowl and mix thoroughly. Cover and leave for 15 minutes or longer in a warm place.

Add the high-grade flour and stir to make a soft dough, adding extra high-grade flour if necessary to make a dough just firm enough to knead.

Knead with the dough hook of an electric mixer or by hand on a lightly floured surface for 10 minutes until the dough forms a soft ball that springs back when gently pressed.

Turn the dough in 2–3 teaspoons of oil in the cleaned dry bowl, cover with cling film and leave in a warm draught-free place for 30 minutes.

Lightly knead the oiled dough in the bowl for 1 minute.

Shaping and Baking

Shape the dough to fit into a loaf pan (see details on page 88) or divide the dough into three. Roll each piece into a 40cm long sausage shape, and place, side by side, on a lightly floured baking sheet lined with baking paper or a Teflon liner. To make a particularly neat braid, start from the middle and plait from the middle to one end, then turn the dough around and plait to the other end (this is a little tricky as you have to work the strands in the opposite order to keep the pattern intact). However, if you prefer, just plait from one end to the other.

Leave to rise in a warm draught-free place for about 1 hour or until the dough has approximately doubled in size.

Spray with water for a crustier braid or brush with milk or egg glaze (page 87). Bake at 200°C for 20–45 minutes (the longer it bakes, the heavier the crust) until the loaf is browned, top and bottom.

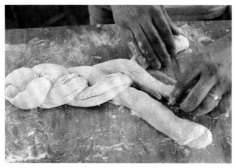

Double Corn Bread

Cornmeal gives this bread a lovely colour, and the creamed corn makes it wonderfully moist and delicious. Try it with or without the herbs, alone, or with your favourite Tex-Mex food.

Makes 1 large loaf:

3 tsp Surebake yeast

½ cup creamed corn

1¼ cups warm water

2 tsp sugar

1½ tsp salt

2 Tbsp lecithin granules or oil

2 cups (280g) high-grade flour

1 cup (140g) wholemeal flour

½ cup fine or coarse cornmeal

½ cup grated cheese

1 tsp each cumin and oregano

pinch of chilli powder

2 Tbsp coarse cornmeal (optional)

Bread Machine Instructions

Carefully measure all the ingredients into a 750g capacity bread machine in the order specified by the manufacturer.

Set to the NORMAL/WHITE bread cycle, MEDIUM crust and START (or use the DOUGH cycle and shape and bake by hand). This is a good timer bread.

Hand-made Bread Instructions

Measure the first six ingredients into a large bowl. Add 1 cup of the high-grade flour and mix thoroughly. Cover and leave for 15 minutes or longer in a warm place.

Add the rest of the high-grade flour along with the remaining ingredients and stir to make a soft dough, adding extra flour if necessary.

Knead with the dough hook of an electric mixer or by hand on a lightly floured surface for 10 minutes, adding extra flour if necessary, until the dough forms a soft ball that springs back when gently pressed.

Turn in 2–3 teaspoons of oil in the cleaned dry bowl, cover with cling film and leave in a warm draught-free place for 30–40 minutes.

Knead the dough in the bowl for 1 minute, then turn out onto a lightly floured surface.

Pat or roll the dough into a square a little larger than the baking pan, then roll into a cylinder. Put into the buttered or sprayed pan, pressing it into the corners and levelling the top.

Leave to rise in a warm draught-free place for about 1 hour or until the dough has approximately doubled in size.

Dampen the top and sprinkle with a little coarse cornmeal if you like, then bake at 200°C for about 30 minutes until the crust is golden, the bottom and sides have browned and the loaf sounds hollow when tapped on the bottom.

Rice Bread

This is a good way to use up left-over cooked rice, which keeps the loaf moist so it stays fresh for several days.

Makes 1 large loaf:

3 tsp Surebake yeast

1¼ cups warm water

2 tsp sugar

1½ tsp salt

2 Tbsp lecithin granules or oil

3 Tbsp non-fat milk powder

1 cup (140g) wholemeal flour

2 cups (280g) high-grade flour

1 cup cooked rice

Bread Machine Instructions

Carefully measure all the ingredients into a 750g capacity bread machine in the order specified by the manufacturer. Add the cooked rice as part of the liquid ingredients. Because the amount of water in the rice may vary, try adding 1 cup rice plus 2 Tbsp of water initially, adding additional water if the dough is too dry. Set to the NORMAL/WHITE bread cycle, MEDIUM crust and START (or use the DOUGH cycle and shape and bake by hand.)

Hand-made Bread Instructions

Measure the first seven ingredients into a large bowl and mix thoroughly. Cover and leave to stand for 15 minutes or longer in a warm place.

Add the high-grade flour and cooked rice, adding a little extra water or enough extra flour to make a soft dough just firm enough to knead.

Knead with the dough hook of an electric mixer or by hand on a lightly floured surface for 10 minutes until the dough is smooth and satiny and springs back when gently pressed.

Turn in 2–3 teaspoons of oil in the cleaned dry bowl, cover with cling film and leave in a warm draught-free place for 30–40 minutes.

Lightly knead the dough in the bowl for 1 minute, then turn out onto a lightly floured surface and pat into a square a little larger than the baking pan. Roll the dough into a cylinder, then put it in the sprayed or buttered pan, pushing it into the corners and levelling the top.

Leave to rise in a warm draught-free place for about 1 hour or until the dough has approximately doubled in size.

If desired, brush with milk or egg glaze (page 87), then bake at 200°C for about 30 minutes or until the bottom and sides have browned and the loaf sounds hollow when tapped.

Potato Bread

Not only does the addition of potato to bread help make it seem more substantial, but it also helps to hold in moisture, keeping the bread fresh for longer.

Bread Machine Instructions

Carefully measure all the ingredients into a 750g capacity bread machine in the order specified by the manufacturer. Set to the NORMAL/WHITE bread cycle, MEDIUM crust and START (or use the DOUGH cycle and shape and rise the loaf by hand as below). This is a good timer bread.

Hand-made Bread Instructions

Measure the first six ingredients into a large bowl and mix thoroughly. Cover and leave for 15 minutes or longer in a warm place.

Stir in the high-grade flour and the potato flakes and stir to make a soft dough, adding a little extra flour if necessary, just firm enough to turn out and knead.

Knead with the dough hook of an electric mixer or by hand on a lightly floured surface for 10 minutes, adding extra flour if necessary.

Turn the dough in 2–3 teaspoons of oil in the cleaned dry bowl, cover with cling film and leave in a warm, draught-free place for 30 minutes.

Shaping and Baking

Lightly knead the oiled dough in the bowl for 1 minute, then gently form it into a large ball. Place on a Teflon or baking paper-lined (or well-oiled) baking sheet and leave to rise again in a warm draught-free place for about 1 hour or until the dough is double in size.

Lightly spray the top of the loaf with water and sprinkle evenly with flour. Cut shallow parallel lines about 2cm apart across the top of the loaf, then repeat at right angles to make a checkerboard pattern.

Bake at 225°C for 20–30 minutes or until the top and bottom is evenly browned and the loaf sounds hollow when tapped underneath.

NOTE: Best eaten when cold as dried potato flakes sometimes give the freshly made bread an unusual flavour that disappears on cooling.

Kumara and Cumin Bread

Kumara and cumin combine to produce a loaf with a lovely moist texture, good keeping qualities, and a very pleasant aroma and flavour.

Bread Machine Instructions

Carefully measure all the ingredients into a 750g capacity bread machine in the order specified by the manufacturer. Set the machine to the NORMAL/WHITE bread setting, MEDIUM crust and START (or use the DOUGH setting and shape and bake as below).

Check the dough after about 5 minutes of mixing. The dough should be a smooth ball – if it looks too wet and sticky, add 1–2 tablespoons of flour and if too dry add similar amounts of water.

Hand-made Bread Instructions

Measure the first nine ingredients into a large bowl. Mix thoroughly, cover, then leave for 15 minutes or longer in a warm place.

Stir in the wholemeal flour, cumin seeds and curry powder. Mix to make a soft dough, adding extra flour if necessary, just firm enough to knead. (You may need to add quite a lot of additional flour, depending on the moisture content of the kumara.)

Knead with the dough hook of an electric mixer or by hand on a lightly floured surface for 10 minutes, adding as much extra flour as necessary to make a soft dough. Turn the dough in 2–3 teaspoons of oil in the cleaned dry bowl, cover with cling film and leave in a warm draught-free place for 30 minutes.

Lightly knead the oiled dough in the bowl for 1 minute.

Shaping and Baking

Divide the dough in half, then pat each piece into a 20x12cm oval shape. Lift onto a lightly sprayed or oiled sponge roll tin, then leave to rise for about 30 minutes or until the loaves are about one and a half times their original size.

Spray with a film of water, then dust with flour (shaken over using a sieve).

Bake at 200°C for 20–35 minutes or until the crust is firm, evenly golden brown, and the loaf or loaves sound hollow when tapped on the bottom.

Five Seed Bread

Five different types of seed are added to this bread which has, as a result, an unusual texture and appearance as well as an interesting flavour.

Makes 1 large loaf (8 cup pan) or 4 small loaves (2 cup pans):

3 tsp Surebake yeast

1¼ cups plus 2 Tbsp warm water

2 tsp sugar

1½ tsp salt

2 Tbsp lecithin granules or oil

1½ cups (210g) high-grade flour

1½ cups (210g) wholemeal flour

¼ cup each sunflower, pumpkin, poppy and raw or toasted sesame seeds*

2 Tbsp linseed

Bread Machine Instructions

Carefully measure all the ingredients into a bread machine in the order specified by the manufacturer. Set to the NORMAL/WHITE cycle, MEDIUM crust and START (or use the DOUGH cycle and shape as below). This is a good timer bread.

Hand-made Bread Instructions

Measure the first six ingredients into a large bowl. Mix thoroughly and then cover and leave for 15 minutes or longer in a warm place.

Stir in the wholemeal flour and the seeds to make a soft dough, adding extra flour if necessary, to make a dough just firm enough to knead.

Knead with the dough hook of an electric mixer or by hand on a lightly floured surface for 10 minutes, adding extra flour if needed.

Turn the dough in 2–3 teaspoons of oil in the cleaned dry bowl, cover with cling film and leave in a warm draught-free place for 30 minutes.

Lightly knead the oiled dough in the bowl for 1 minute.

Shaping and Baking

Pat the dough into a square a little larger than the baking pan. Roll the dough into a cylinder, then press into the buttered or sprayed pan, pressing it into the corners and levelling the top. If using small pans, divide the dough into four, then shape each piece as above.

Leave to rise in a warm draught-free place for about 1 hour or until double its original size.

If desired, brush with milk or egg glaze (page 87), then sprinkle with any of the seeds used in the loaf.

Bake at 200°C for 15–35 minutes or until the bottom and sides are browned and the loaf sounds hollow when tapped.

*For maximum flavour, toast sesame seeds in a dry frypan or under the grill before using them.

Muesli Bread

Try muesli on a bread and butter plate for a change! This is a great breakfast bread, slightly sweet, with good flavour and texture.

Makes 1 large loaf (6–8 cup pan):

3 tsp Surebake yeast

1½ cups warm water

2 Tbsp sugar

1 tsp salt

2 Tbsp lecithin granules or oil

1 cup (140g) wholemeal flour

2 cups (280g) high-grade flour

1 cup toasted muesli

Bread Machine Instructions

Carefully measure all the ingredients into a 750g capacity bread machine in the order specified by the manufacturer.

Set to the NORMAL/WHITE bread cycle, MEDIUM crust and START (or use the DOUGH cycle and shape by hand). This is a good timer bread.

Hand-made Bread Instructions

Measure the first six ingredients into a large bowl. Mix thoroughly, then cover and leave for 15 minutes or longer in a warm place.

Stir in the high-grade flour and muesli to make a soft dough. Add enough high-grade flour to make a dough just firm enough to knead.

Knead with the dough hook of an electric mixer or by hand on a floured surface for 10 minutes, adding extra flour if necessary.

Turn the dough in 2–3 teaspoons of oil in the cleaned dry bowl, cover with cling film and leave in a warm draught-free place for about 30 minutes.

Knead the oiled dough in the bowl for 1 minute, pat into a square a little larger than the baking pan, then roll into a cylinder and put into the oiled or sprayed bread pan, pressing it into the corners and levelling the top. For something different, shape into rolls, a braid or a round cottage loaf (page 88).

Leave to rise in a warm, draught-free place for about 1 hour or until double its original size.

If desired, brush with milk or egg glaze (page 87), sprinkle with sunflower or other seeds, and bake at 200°C–210°C for about 30 minutes until the sides and bottom are golden brown and the loaf sounds hollow when tapped underneath.

Raisin and Nut Bread

The addition of cinnamon, raisins and a handful of nuts make this bread something quite special. If you want to fill the house with a wonderful aroma that's great to wake up to, try it with cinnamon as well.

**Makes 1 large loaf
(6–8 cup pan):**

3 tsp Surebake yeast

1¼ cups plus 2 Tbsp
warm water

2 Tbsp sugar

1 tsp salt

2 Tbsp lecithin
granules or oil

2 Tbsp non-fat milk
powder

1½ cups (210g)
high-grade flour

1½ cups (210g)
wholemeal flour

2 tsp cinnamon (optional)

½ cup raisins

¼ cup chopped nuts,
e.g. walnuts or pecans

Bread Machine Instructions

Carefully measure all the ingredients into a 750g capacity bread machine in the order specified by the manufacturer.

Set to the RAISIN BREAD (FRUIT LOAF) cycle, MEDIUM crust and START, adding the nuts and raisins when the machine beeps. This is a good timer bread. If using the timer, just place the raisins and nuts on top of everything else.

Hand-made Bread Instructions

Measure the first seven ingredients into a large bowl and mix thoroughly. Cover and leave for 15 minutes or longer in a warm place.

Stir in the wholemeal flour and the cinnamon, if using, and the raisins and nuts. Add extra flour if necessary to make a dough just firm enough to knead.

Knead with the dough hook of an electric mixer or by hand on a lightly floured surface for 10 minutes, adding extra flour if necessary.

Turn the dough in 2–3 teaspoons of oil in the cleaned dry bowl, cover with cling film and leave in a warm draught-free place for 30 minutes.

Lightly knead the oiled dough in the bowl for 1 minute, then pat it into a square a little larger than the baking pan. Roll the dough into a cylinder, then put into the oiled or sprayed pan, pressing it into the corners and levelling the top.

Leave to rise in a warm draught-free place for about 1 hour or until doubled in size.

If desired, brush with milk or with egg glaze (page 87) and bake at 200°C for about 30 minutes or until the sides and bottom are browned and the loaf sounds hollow when tapped underneath.

Fruity Oat Bread

This is a delicious fruity loaf with a golden brown crumb and a wonderful flavour that will appeal to everyone who likes the combination of almonds and fruit.

**Makes 1 medium-large
loaf (6–8 cup pan):**

3 tsp Surebake yeast

1¼ cups warm water

1 large egg

1 Tbsp honey

1 tsp salt

3 Tbsp lecithin
granules or oil

3 Tbsp non-fat milk
powder

1 cup (140g)
wholemeal flour

2 cups (280g)
high-grade flour

1 cup rolled oats

½ cup each chopped
dried apricots and
Californian raisins

¼ cup slivered almonds,
toasted

Bread Machine Instructions

Carefully measure all the ingredients into a 750g capacity bread machine in the order specified by the manufacturer.

Set to the NORMAL/WHITE bread cycle, MEDIUM crust and START (or use the DOUGH cycle and shape and bake by hand as described below).

Hand-made Bread Instructions

Measure the first eight ingredients into a large bowl and stir until smooth, then cover and leave for 15 minutes or longer in a warm place.

Add the high-grade flour, rolled oats and the dried fruit and nuts. Stir together to make a soft dough, adding a little extra warm water or flour if necessary.

Knead with the dough hook of an electric mixer or by hand on a lightly floured surface for 10 minutes, adding extra flour if necessary.

Turn the dough in 1–2 teaspoons of oil in the cleaned dry bowl. Cover with cling film and leave in a warm draught-free place for 30–40 minutes.

Lightly knead the oiled dough in the bowl for 1 minute, then form into a rectangle a little longer than the baking pan. Roll the dough into a cylinder and place in the sprayed or oiled pan, pressing it into the corners and levelling the top.

Leave to rise in a warm draught-free place for about 1 hour or until the dough has approximately doubled in size.

Bake at 180°C for 30–40 minutes until the sides and bottom are golden brown and the loaf sounds hollow when tapped underneath.

Remove from the oven and brush with golden syrup glaze (page 87), if desired.

Bagels

Let the plane to New York leave without you! Make your own wonderfully chewy bagels for about a tenth of the price of bought ones in a surprisingly short time. Spoil yourself with traditional toppings of cream cheese and smoked salmon. Bliss!

Makes 8 plump bagels:

3 tsp Surebake yeast

1¼ cups warm water

2 Tbsp honey

1½ tsp salt

1 cup (140g) wholemeal flour

2 Tbsp gluten flour

2 cups (280g) high-grade flour

Bread Machine Instructions

Carefully measure all the ingredients into a 750g capacity bread machine in the order specified by the manufacturer.

Set to the DOUGH cycle and START. Stop the machine and remove the dough 40 minutes after mixing starts, even though the cycle is not complete.

Shape and bake by hand following the instructions below.

Hand-made Bread Instructions

Measure the first five ingredients into a large bowl and mix thoroughly. Cover and leave for 15 minutes or longer in a warm place.

Stir in the gluten and high-grade flour, adding extra flour or water if necessary, until you have a dough just firm enough to knead.

Knead with the dough hook of an electric mixer or by hand on a lightly floured surface for 10 minutes until you have a soft, smooth, satiny dough that springs back when gently pressed.

Turn the dough in 2–3 teaspoons of oil in the cleaned dry bowl. Cover with cling film and leave in a warm draught-free place for 30 minutes.

Shaping and Baking

Lightly knead the dough for 1 minute, then cut into eight equal pieces. Roll each into a 26cm long "snake". Working with one length at a time, dampen each end with water and press together firmly to form a ring. Place the rings on a sheet of oiled baking paper and leave for 10–15 minutes.

Meanwhile, bring a large pan containing 5–10cm water to the boil. Carefully lower three bagels at a time into the boiling water (slide them into the water from the paper to avoid burning your hands), lift away the paper, and cook for 30–45 seconds per side. Drain on paper towels, then put the bagels on a large baking sheet lined with baking paper or a Teflon liner, leaving space between them for rising.

Brush as far down the sides as you can with egg glaze (page 87) and sprinkle with poppy or toasted sesame seeds.

Bake at 220°C for 10–12 minutes until browned top and bottom. Cool on a rack and serve warm or toasted within 24 hours of making or freeze in an airtight container as soon as they are cold.

Croissants

Everybody's favourite! Although the recipe may seem complicated at first, once you have made these a few times you will become a dab hand. Follow the instructions carefully, rolling and folding the dough to produce light flaky layers.

Makes 10–12 croissants:

3 tsp Surebake yeast

1 cup warm water

1 large egg

25g butter, melted

2 tsp sugar

1 tsp salt

¼ cup non-fat milk powder

3–3½ cups (420-490g) high-grade flour

100–150g cold butter

Bread Machine Instructions

Add all the ingredients except the second measure of butter to a 750g capacity bread machine in the order specified by the manufacturer.

Set to the DOUGH cycle and START. When the dough is completed, remove it from the machine, place in a plastic bag and refrigerate for 10–15 minutes before proceeding as below.

Hand-made Dough Instructions

Measure the first seven ingredients into a large bowl. Add 1½ cups of the measured flour and mix thoroughly. Cover, then leave to stand for 15 minutes or longer in a warm place.

Stir in the remaining flour to make a soft dough, adding more flour if necessary, until just firm enough to knead.

Knead with the dough hook of an electric mixer or by hand on a lightly floured surface for 10 minutes, adding extra flour if necessary, until the dough forms a soft ball that springs back when gently pressed.

Place in a plastic bag and refrigerate for 10–15 minutes.

Layering and Baking Instructions

While the dough cools, prepare the cold butter by placing it between two sheets of plastic or cling film. Using a rolling pin, roll the butter into a 10x15cm rectangle of 5–7mm thickness, then remove the plastic.

From this stage keep everything as cold as possible.

Turn out the chilled dough onto a lightly floured board and roll into a 25x35cm rectangle. Lay the sheet of butter diagonally across the rectangle (see diagram), then fold the corners of the dough over the butter so it is completely contained in an envelope of dough.

Place on a tray and refrigerate for 15 minutes.

Fold the chilled dough in half so the short ends meet, then roll gently into a 30x20cm rectangle.

Next, fold the dough into thirds (see diagram) as you would fold a sheet of paper to put into an envelope, and refrigerate for 10 minutes.

Once again roll out the chilled dough into a 30x20cm rectangle, then fold into thirds as above. Roll out to the original size and fold in thirds once more before refrigerating for another 10 minutes.

Cut the dough in half lengthwise and return half to the refrigerator. Roll the other half into a 40x20cm rectangle. Using a sharp knife, make diagonal cuts across the dough (see diagram) to make five or six fairly even triangles.

Starting with the short side of the dough triangle facing towards you, roll up each shape loosely, moistening the pointed end with a little cold water to seal it down.

Bend the pointed ends inwards to form the traditional croissant shape and lie them (with the pointed tips underneath) on a buttered or sprayed baking sheet, allowing plenty of room for spreading.

Repeat this process, making another five or six croissants in the same way with the remaining dough, and put these on another baking sheet.

Leave to rise in a warm draught-free place for 1–2 hours (or overnight in the refrigerator) until double their original volume.

Brush with egg glaze (page 87) and bake at 200°C for 15–20 minutes until golden brown on the top and underneath.

Cool on a rack. Serve warm with your favourite jam (and butter if you like) or split and add your favourite fillings for lunch.

Brioche

Brioche are very versatile and can be enjoyed with coffee and jam for breakfast or served as rich dinner rolls.

Makes 8–10 brioche:

½ cup warm milk

3 large eggs

3 tsp Surebake yeast

¼ cup sugar

1 tsp salt

3 cups (420g) standard plain flour plus ¼ cup if required

75g butter, melted

Bread Machine Instructions

Carefully measure all the ingredients into a 750g capacity bread machine in the order specified by the manufacturer. Set to the DOUGH cycle, and START. Check the dough after about 3 minutes of mixing. It should be soft, but if it looks too wet and sticky add 2 tablespoons of the extra flour (repeat if necessary).

When the dough cycle is complete, remove the dough from the machine and transfer to a well-oiled bowl. Refrigerate for at least 1 hour (or overnight), then shape and bake as below.

Hand-made Bread Instructions

In a large bowl mix together the warm milk and eggs. Sprinkle on the yeast and leave to stand for 5 minutes. Add the sugar, salt and 1½ cups of flour, and mix thoroughly. Cover and leave for 15 minutes or longer in a warm place.

Add the butter and the remaining flour, then stir to make a soft dough, adding a little extra flour if necessary.

Knead with the dough hook of an electric mixer or by hand on a lightly floured surface for 10 minutes.

Turn in 2–3 teaspoons of oil in the cleaned dry bowl, cover with cling film and refrigerate for at least 1 hour (or overnight).

Shaping and Baking

Turn out the dough on a lightly floured surface and divide into four or five pieces, then halve each to give a total of eight or 10 equal pieces. Shape each piece into a ball, then with the side of your hand almost saw off quarter of the dough. Pick up each ball by the smaller part and place in a well-oiled muffin pan or fluted brioche pan. Press the smaller ball firmly onto the base so that each one looks like a small snowman.

Leave to rise in a warm draught-free place for about 1 hour or until the dough is approximately double in size.

Brush with egg glaze (page 87) and bake at 180°C for about 15 minutes or until golden brown on all surfaces.

Danish Pastries

Danish pastries are made from croissant dough which may be shaped in many ways to make these flaky, luxurious treats for weekend breakfasts and brunches.

To make the almond filling, beat together with a fork 1 egg white or yolk (or half an egg), ½ cup ground almonds, ¼ cup sugar and a few drops of almond essence.

To make custard, mix together until smooth 2 tablespoons each sugar and cornflour, ¾ cup milk and 1 egg. Heat gently until thick, stirring all the time, then add 1 teaspoon butter. Allow to cool before using.

Almond Danish Pastries

Roll out all the croissant dough to form a 36cm square. Trim the edges straight, then cut into nine 12cm squares.

Put no more than 1 tablespoon of almond filling in the middle of each square, then fold each corner over the filling and into the middle of the pastry, so the corners overlap slightly. Press the centre and outer edges firmly. Place each pastry in an individual pie pan if you have them, otherwise on a lightly floured baking sheet.

Bake at 200°C for 15–20 minutes or until evenly browned. If you like, place a canned apricot half or other piece of fruit in the centre of each after about 10 minutes. Brush the cooked pastries while very hot with some sieved heated apricot jam or apricot glaze.

Apple-filled "Snails"

Roll out the croissant dough to form two rectangles each about 20x40cm. Spread each with the almond filling or with custard, leaving 2–3cm clear on one long side.

Over the almond filling or cold custard, spread about 1 cup well-drained stewed apple, ¼ cup sugar and ½ cup sultanas. Moisten the uncovered edges with water and roll up, dampened edges last. Cut each roll into 12–18 pinwheels or snails, place on baking-paper lined baking sheets, in individual round pie pans, or arrange in baking-paper lined cake pans as for Cinnamon Swirls, page 64, then leave to rise at room temperature for 1–2 hours (or overnight in the refrigerator).

Bake at 200°C for about 15 minutes. Brush while very hot with sieved heated apricot jam or apricot glaze.

Quick English Muffins

These are made from a soft yeast dough and cooked with cornmeal to stop them sticking to any surface which they touch.

For 8 English Muffins:

25g butter

¾ cup boiling water

½ cup milk

1 Tbsp granulated yeast

2 tsp sugar

2½–3 cups (350-420g) plain flour

1 tsp salt

about ¼ cup cornmeal

Bread Machine Instructions

Measure the butter into the bread machine, pour in the boiling water then leave to stand until the butter has melted before adding the milk, yeast, sugar and 2½ cups (350g) of flour, set the machine to the DOUGH cycle and press START. Shape and cook as described below.

Hand-made Bread Instructions

Measure the butter into a large bowl. Pour the boiling water over the butter, then add the cold milk. Sprinkle in the yeast and sugar then stir until yeast dissolves. Leave to stand in a warm place for 5-10 minutes, until the surface bubbles. Add 2½ cups of flour and salt and beat to mix thoroughly. Leave to stand in a warm place until mixture doubles in size (about 30 minutes).

Shaping and Cooking

Stir the mixture back to original size, then turn it onto a well-floured board adding just enough extra flour so you can work with it without it sticking. Keeping dough very soft, adding as little flour as possible, cut it into eight pieces and roll into balls using well-floured hands. Roll the balls in cornmeal (to stop them sticking), then place each one on a 10cm square of sprayed or oiled lunch paper or plastic wrap and leave to rise in a warm place for 15–20 minutes, until light and puffy.

Carefully place muffins, paper side up and top side down, into an electric frypan or griddle which has been preheated to 150°C, then lift off the plastic or paper. Cook muffins for about 2 minutes, then carefully turn. Cook second side for 5–7 minutes, turn again and cook for a further 5 minutes. (This produces muffins with even-sized cooked surfaces.)

Turn onto a rack to cool and store in the refrigerator.

Before serving, brown each side under the grill, then split and eat while hot with your favourite sweet or savoury topping. Alternatively, split the muffins, then brown in toaster.

Crumpets

Crumpets are a bit like pikelets risen with yeast instead of baking powder. They have tunnels which run from bottom to top and a special, different texture because they are made from a very runny dough. Our homemade crumpets aren't exactly the same as bought ones, but they're very good and fun to make.

For about 10 Crumpets:

1½ cups hot water

1 cup milk

1 Tbsp granulated yeast

1 tsp sugar

2 cups (280g) plain flour

1 tsp salt

Mixing in a Bread Machine

Measure all the ingredients into the bread machine. Set to the PIZZA (or shortest cycle) and press START. Stop the machine after about 20 minutes of mixing, but leave the batter to stand in the machine for another 15-20 minutes. Cook as described below.

Mixing By Hand Instructions

Mix the hot water and milk together in a large bowl. Sprinkle in the yeast and sugar and leave to stand in a warm place until the surface bubbles, usually 5-10 minutes. Measure the flour and salt into a microwavable bowl and heat it on High (100% power) in 10 second bursts, until it feels warm (2 cups of flour takes 20-30 seconds). Add the warmed flour and salt to the yeast mixture and stir vigorously for several minutes. Cover the bowl with plastic film and leave to stand in a warm place for about 30 minutes, until mixture is bubbly and has doubled in size. Do not stir the risen mixture.

Cooking

Heat a well-buttered or sprayed frypan to 150°C, or a griddle to a temperature lower than you would use for cooking pikelets. Also spray or butter some 10cm metal rings (you can buy egg rings or use small cans with both ends cut out). Place rings in frypan (or on the griddle) and spoon in enough dough to fill the ring 1cm deep.

Cook the crumpets for about 5 minutes. As the crumpets cook, bubbles rise up and burst, leaving tunnels. After 3-4 minutes, the edges should be cooked and you will probably be able to remove the baking ring. Turn the crumpets when the top is set, and cook for 1–2 minutes to dry the surface. Place on a rack to cool. Before serving crumpets, brown both sides under a grill or in a toaster. Eat while hot, topped with butter and golden or maple syrup, honey or jam.

Naan

Although we like all the Indian flat breads we have tried, naan is our favourite. We are just as happy to eat naan with a barbecue as we are with a curry – in fact, we like them with almost any meal.

Makes 8 naan breads:

3 tsp Surebake yeast

¾ cup warm water plus 2 Tbsp

¼ cup plain unsweetened yoghurt

50g butter, melted

1 tsp sugar

1 tsp salt

1 cup (140g) wholemeal flour

2 cups (280g) high-grade flour

extra butter, melted, or oil

sesame or cumin seeds (optional)

Bread Machine Instructions

Carefully measure all the ingredients into a 750g capacity bread machine in the order specified by the manufacturer.

Set to the DOUGH cycle and START. When the dough is ready, tip out onto a lightly floured surface and follow the instructions for shaping and baking below.

Hand-made Bread Instructions

Measure the first seven ingredients into a large bowl and mix well. Cover and leave for 15 minutes or longer in a warm place.

Stir in the high-grade flour, adding a little extra warm water or flour if necessary to make a dough just firm enough to knead.

Knead with the dough hook of an electric mixer or by hand on a lightly floured surface for 10 minutes. Try to keep the dough as soft as you can as a soft dough produces good naan, adding a little extra water if it is too firm, and a touch of extra flour if it is too soft to work with. After kneading, the dough should form a soft ball that springs back when gently pressed.

Turn the dough in 2 teaspoons of oil in the cleaned dry bowl, cover with cling film and leave in a warm draught-free place for 30 minutes.

Turn out the dough and lightly knead for about 1 minute.

Shaping and Baking

Divide the dough into four pieces, then halve each piece to give eight balls. Cover and leave to stand for 5 minutes.

Roll out each ball into a flat oval shape about 18cm wide and 22–23cm long. Brush each side with the extra melted butter or oil. Sprinkle with sesame or cumin seeds if you like.

Heat the oven to 225°C–250°C. If you have one, place a cast-iron pan or griddle on the rack just below the middle (this will heat up and compensate for heat loss when the oven door is opened). Place one bread at a time on the very hot pan and cook for about 4 minutes (turning after 2 minutes) until puffed and lightly browned on both sides. Alternatively, cook the naan bread on the hot plate of your barbecue, turning once as above.

Eat soon after baking.

Chocolate Hot Cross Buns

We like traditional, fruit and spice flavoured hot cross buns, but for some reason Simon's children have gone off them, and now prefer this chocolate version.

Makes 16 hot cross buns:

3 tsp instant active yeast

½ cup milk

¾ cup hot water

½ cup brown sugar

½ tsp salt

50g butter, melted

1 large egg

½ cup cocoa powder

4 cups (560g) high-grade flour

½ cup chocolate chips

Bread Machine Instructions

Measure all the ingredients into a 750g capacity bread machine in the order specified by the manufacturer. Set to the DOUGH cycle and START. (Add the chocolate chips at the beep if your machine offers this option). When the cycle is complete, shape and bake as below.

Hand-made Bread Instructions

Measure the yeast, milk, hot water, 1 tablespoon of the brown sugar and the salt into a large bowl. Stir after 2 minutes to ensure the yeast has dissolved before adding 2 cups of the measured high-grade flour. Cover and leave in a warm place for about 30 minutes.

In another bowl mix together the melted butter and remaining brown sugar, then beat in the egg. Add the risen yeast mixture and the cocoa powder and remaining flour and mix to make a dough just firm enough to knead, adding a little extra flour if necessary.

Knead with the dough hook of an electric mixer or by hand on a lightly floured surface for 10 minutes. Add the chocolate chips and knead for 1 minute longer. Shape and bake as below.

Shaping and Baking

Divide the dough evenly into four pieces, then again into four quarters so you have 16 pieces in total. Shape each one into a round ball and arrange in non-stick sprayed (and/or baking paper-lined) baking pans or in a rectangular roasting dish, leaving about 1cm between each bun. Cover with cling film and leave in a warm place until doubled in size.

If you want to add pastry crosses, use the method in the next recipe. Alternatively, bake the buns first and decorate when cooled with crosses made with vanilla or chocolate icing or melted white or dark chocolate.

Bake at 200°C for 12–15 minutes or until lightly browned. Glaze immediately with a syrup made by bringing to the boil 1 tablespoon each golden syrup, honey and water.

Hot Cross Buns

A wonderful treat for Easter (or any time for that matter!), home-made hot cross buns are well worth the effort. When time is short, make Easter buns (i.e. buns without crosses).

To make 16–20 Hot Cross Buns:

½ cup each warm milk and water

½ cup brown sugar

4 tsp active dried yeast

4 cups (560g) high-grade flour

75g butter, barely melted

1 large egg

1 tsp salt

1 Tbsp each mixed spice and cinnamon

1 tsp each ground cloves and vanilla essence

1 cup mixed fruit or currants

Bread Machine Instructions

Carefully measure all the ingredients into a 750g capacity bread machine in the order specified by the manufacturer. Set to the DOUGH cycle and START. (Add the mixed fruit at the beep if your machine offers this option.) When the cycle is complete, shape and bake as below.

Hand-made Bread Instructions

Measure the warm milk, water and 1 tablespoon of the brown sugar into a large bowl, warm or cool the mixture to body temperature, then sprinkle in the yeast granules. Stir after 2 minutes to ensure yeast has dissolved before adding 2 cups of the measured high-grade flour. Cover and leave in a warm place for about 30 minutes.

In another bowl mix together the melted butter and remaining brown sugar, then beat in the egg, salt, spices, vanilla essence and dried fruit. Add the risen yeast mixture and the remaining high-grade flour and mix to make a dough just firm enough to knead, adding a little extra flour if necessary.

Knead with the dough hook of an electric mixer or by hand on a lightly floured surface for 10 minutes.

Shaping and Baking

Divide the dough evenly into four pieces, then again into four or five so you have 16 or 20 pieces in total. Shape each piece into a round ball (page 21) and arrange in sprayed or Teflon-lined baking pans or in a rectangular roasting dish, leaving about 1cm between each bun. Cover with cling film and leave in a warm place until doubled in size.

If you want to add pastry crosses, rub 60g cold butter into 1 cup high-grade flour, then add about 3 tablespoons cold water to form a stiff dough. Roll out very thinly then cut into strips, brush with beaten egg and place carefully on the risen buns, egg side down.

Bake at 225°C for 10–12 minutes or until lightly browned. Glaze immediately with a syrup made by bringing to the boil 1 tablespoon each golden syrup, honey and water.

Festive Wreath

This wreath is something really special. It may seem rather complicated the first time you try it, but we think that it will be received so enthusiastically that you will want to make it again. Simplify the shaping if you like.

Makes a 35–40cm wreath:

Dough:

3 tsp active dried yeast

1¼ cups warm milk

1 Tbsp sugar

1½ tsp salt

50g butter, softened

3 cups (420g) standard plain flour

Filling:

50g butter

2 Tbsp sugar

¼ cup standard plain flour

¾ tsp almond essence

½ cup each toasted slivered almonds and chopped dried apricots

¼ cup each red and green glacé cherries, chopped

Bread Machine Instructions

Carefully measure all the dough ingredients into a 750g capacity bread machine in the order specified by the manufacturer.

Set to the DOUGH cycle and START. When the cycle is complete, remove the dough and fill, shape and bake as described below.

Hand-made Bread Instructions

Measure the first five ingredients into a large bowl with 1½ cups of the flour. Mix thoroughly, then cover and leave for 15 minutes or longer in a warm place.

Add the remaining flour and stir to make a soft dough, adding a little extra flour if necessary, just firm enough to knead. Knead with the dough hook of an electric mixer or by hand on a lightly floured surface for 10 minutes, adding extra flour if necessary, until the dough forms a soft ball that springs back when gently pressed.

Turn the dough in 2 teaspoons of oil in the cleaned dry bowl, cover with cling film and leave in a warm draught-free place for 30–40 minutes.

Filling, Shaping and Baking

Prepare the filling by beating together the softened butter, sugar, flour and essence, then fold in the fruit and nuts.

Lightly knead the dough for 1 minute, then roll out into a 25x70cm rectangle on a well-floured surface.

Dot the filling evenly over the dough, then roll up tightly starting from a long edge. Using a sharp knife cut the roll in half lengthwise, then twist the two strands loosely together, cut sides out. Form into a ring, pinching the ends together, on a floured baking sheet. Leave to rise in a warm, draught-free place for 40–60 minutes or until double its original size.

Brush lightly with egg glaze (page 87) and bake at 200°C for 20 minutes or until lightly browned.

Remove from the oven and cool on a rack. If you like, drizzle while warm with icing made by mixing until smooth 1 cup sifted icing sugar with 2 tablespoons lemon juice.

Cinnamon Swirls

The warm, inviting smell of yeast and cinnamon wafting through the house as these rolls cook is a promise of a treat to come. Reward your family after they have finished all the jobs you want done.

Makes about 12 rolls:

2 tsp Surebake yeast

½ cup milk

2 Tbsp warm water

1 Tbsp sugar

1 tsp salt

25g butter, melted

2 cups (280g) high-grade flour

Filling:

1-2 Tbsp butter, melted

½ cup brown sugar

1 tsp cinnamon

2 Tbsp chopped walnuts

Topping:

2 Tbsp butter, softened

2 Tbsp brown sugar

2 Tbsp chopped walnuts

Bread Machine Instructions

Carefully measure all the ingredients into a 750g capacity bread machine in the order specified by the manufacturer.

Set to the DOUGH cycle and START. When the dough is ready, tip it out onto a lightly floured surface and follow the instructions for shaping and baking below.

Hand-made Bread Instructions

Measure the first six ingredients into a bowl with half the flour. Cover and leave to stand for 15 minutes in a warm place.

Stir in the remaining flour with a little extra flour or water if necessary to make a dough just firm enough to knead.

Knead with the dough hook of an electric mixer or by hand on a lightly floured surface for 10 minutes or until the dough forms a soft ball that springs back when gently pressed.

Turn in 2 teaspoons of oil in the cleaned dry bowl, cover with cling film and leave in a warm draught-free place for 30–40 minutes.

Lightly knead the dough in the bowl for 1 minute.

Shaping and Baking

Rub 2 tablespoons of soft butter fairly evenly over the bottom and up the sides of a 20–23cm round cake pan, then sprinkle 2 tablespoons each brown sugar and chopped walnuts over the bottom.

Roll out the dough to form a square, about 30x30cm then brush it lightly with a little melted butter. Sprinkle with ½ cup brown sugar, 1 teaspoon cinnamon, and 2 tablespoons chopped walnuts if you like.

Roll up to form a cylinder, then cut into about eight to12 fairly even slices. (Make the larger number for the larger pan.) Arrange them, cut side down, as evenly as you can in the prepared cake pan, leaving space around each roll to spread. Cover with cling film and leave to rise in a warm draught-free place for about 1 hour or until twice the original size.

Bake at 180°C for 20–30 minutes or until golden brown. Carefully turn the loaf out of the pan onto a plate or board straight away and serve warm.

Sweet dough breads

It seems quite magical that one basic dough can be shaped into so many different treats. Once you feel at home with yeast doughs, experiment using other basic doughs from this book in similar ways. Eat your goodies the day you make them!

Basic Sweet Dough

2 tsp Surebake yeast

1 cup plus 2 Tbsp water

1 large egg

3 Tbsp lecithin granules or butter

¼ cup sugar

1 tsp salt

¼ cup non-fat milk powder

3 cups (420g) high-grade flour

Bread Machine Instructions

Carefully measure all the ingredients into a 750g capacity bread machine in the order specified by the manufacturer.

Set to the DOUGH cycle and START. When the cycle is complete, take out the dough and shape and bake as below.

Hand-made Bread Instructions

Measure the first seven ingredients into a large bowl with 1½ cups of the high-grade flour and mix thoroughly. Cover and leave for 15 minutes or longer in a warm place.

Stir in the remaining flour to make a soft dough, adding a little extra warm water or flour if necessary, just firm enough to turn out and knead.

Knead the dough with the dough hook of an electric mixer or by hand on a lightly floured surface for 10 minutes until the dough forms a non-sticky soft ball that springs back when gently pressed.

Turn the dough in 2–3 teaspoons of oil in the cleaned dry bowl, cover with cling film and leave in a warm draught-free place for 30 minutes.

Lightly knead the oiled dough in the bowl for 1 minute, then shape as required.

After shaping, leave to rise again for 30–60 minutes in a warm, draught-free place until risen to about one and a half times its original size.

French Braid

To make a 30cm fruit braid, use half the dough. (Refrigerate the rest in a plastic bag, punching it down if it rises a lot before you are ready to use it.)

On a strip of baking paper, roll the dough into an oval shape measuring about 20x30cm. Mark into three equal strips, then cut the two outer thirds into about 10 flaps (see page 89).

For a filling, mix together about ½ cup of either Christmas mincemeat, lemon honey or jam with 2 tablespoons cake or biscuit crumbs or coconut or make this apricot filling. Heat together ½ cup chopped dried apricots and ¼ cup orange juice until the liquid is absorbed. Add ¼ cup chopped almonds, 2 tablespoons each coconut and sugar and mix well. Cool.

Spread the cold filling evenly down the centre section of the dough. Tuck the ends in, then fold alternating strips over the filling much as if you were plaiting it. The plaited braid should have an even shape, so taper it in once you pass the middle. Tuck the ends of the last two pieces underneath, making the end as neat as possible.

Slide the baking paper holding the braid onto a baking sheet. Leave to rise as in the basic recipe. Brush with milk or egg glaze (page 87), then bake at 200°C for about 15 minutes or until golden brown on the top and bottom. If you like, drizzle with icing (page 63) while warm, and decorate with nuts or chopped cherries.

Cream Buns

To make 12–18 cream buns: divide the dough into 12–18 pieces, each about 50g, and shape into even rolls making sure that their tops are smooth (Yoghurt Bread page 21).

Place the shaped rolls on baking paper in a large roasting dish or other high-sided pan and cover with cling film or stand the pan in a large plastic bag, and leave to rise as described in the basic recipe.

Brush with milk or egg glaze (page 87), then bake at 200°C for 10–12 minutes or until golden brown. Cool on a rack, then cut diagonally leaving a hinge. When cooled to room temperature, fill with a spoonful of raspberry or other jam, and some plain or lightly sweetened whipped cream. Dust with icing sugar just before serving if you like.

Fruit Buns

Make the Basic Sweet Dough, adding ½–1 cup currants, sultanas, raisins, mixed fruit or a mixture of finely chopped dried apricots and other dried fruits to the dough at the time when the bread machine beeps or, if making by hand, when the last measure of flour is added.

Shape buns as for Cream Buns. Bake without glazing. As soon as the buns are cooked, brush while still very hot with golden syrup glaze (page 87).

Doughnuts

To make 16–18 doughnuts: on a lightly floured surface roll out the basic sweet dough until about 1cm thick. Using a doughnut cutter or a 7cm round biscuit cutter, cut out circles, re-rolling the scraps to make more. With a 2cm cutter cut out the centre of each doughnut. (Keep these off-cuts to cook at the same time as the doughnuts, since they are very popular with small children.)

Put each doughnut on a square of baking paper and leave to rise until nearly doubled in size.

Heat about 5cm of oil in a frypan, wok or deep-fryer. (It will be hot enough when a scrap of dough turns golden brown in about 15 seconds.) Cook doughnuts one or two at a time, turning to cook the other side before lifting them out and leaving to drain on paper towels. (The off-cuts should cook in about 45 seconds.)

Toss each drained, cooled doughnut in a plastic bag with 1–2 teaspoons cinnamon sugar (made by mixing ¼ cup caster sugar with 1 teaspoon cinnamon). These are best eaten within half an hour of cooking.

No Knead
BREAD

"No Knead" Bread Basics

"No knead" bread is quite a revolutionary idea! The next five recipes call for mixing a ball of dough which is too wet to knead traditionally. After it has been left to stand in its bowl until it is double its size, you shape part of, or all the dough you want to cook today, very gently, into rolls or loaves, with very floury hands. (The rest of the dough is refrigerated for several days in the refrigerator and used as you want it.) It seems like magic but it works!

Really Easy "No Knead" Bread

Here is a really easy and very good bread, made without any kneading. For this bread, five ingredients are stirred together in a large bowl. The first shaped and baked chewy rolls should be ready to eat a little more than an hour after you start mixing! The rest of the dough, refrigerated in its bowl, may be taken out, shaped in any way you like, and baked at any times that suit you during the next four days!

2 cups of body-temperature water

2 tsp Surebake yeast

1 Tbsp olive or canola oil

2 tsp salt

4 cups (about 560g) high-grade white flour

Measure the warm (body-temperature) water into a large bowl. Sprinkle the yeast over the water, stir it in, then add the oil and the salt.

Stir the flour in its bag to aerate it, then fork or spoon the flour lightly into a measuring cup and level off the top. Tip this flour into the bowl and stir it into the liquid using a large flexible stirrer or a wooden spoon. Repeat with three more cups of flour, stirring again after each one is added. At the end of this time the mixture should have formed a rather sticky ball of dough. If it seems too liquid, add about an extra quarter cup of flour and beat again until a sticky ball forms. Dampen the stirrer or a scraper and use it to clean down the sides of the bowl.

Cover the bowl of dough and leave it to stand in a warm place until the dough has risen to about twice its original size, usually in 15–20 minutes. Heat the oven to 230°C with a rack just above the middle.

For rolls which you can eat very soon, using about one quarter of the dough, tilt the bowl of risen dough and let about quarter of the

dough fall out onto a well-floured surface. You will need to cut off the amount of dough you want, using a wetted knife or a rectangular metal dough cutter. Cover and refrigerate the rest of the dough in the covered bowl.

Gently turn the soft dough over so that all its sides are floured. (It will be softer than traditional, firmer bread dough which has been kneaded.) Pat the soft dough out into a rectangle with floured hands, then fold the ends over again, and pat it down into a rectangular shape again. Cut the rectangle of soft (folded) dough into 4–8 more or less triangular rolls using the dough cutter or a heavy knife. (We like it if the rolls have irregular shapes.)

Put the shaped rolls on a floured baking tray, leaving space for rising, and leave them to stand (and rise again) for about 15 minutes (or up to 45 minutes if you are not impatient!)

Bake the rolls for 15–20 minutes, until golden brown, then cool on a rack. The crust becomes thicker with longer cooking.

"No Knead" Round Crusty Loaves

Make this really easy dough by mixing together only four basic ingredients. You can then use some or all of the dough straight away, or you can refrigerate the big ball of dough for up to a week, cutting off and baking half, or a quarter of the original dough whenever it suits you. Each half of the dough makes a round loaf, weighing about 650g, and each quarter of the dough makes a smaller round loaf which weighs about 325g.

We had some trouble with the loaves we made initially. Although we really liked their open texture and good flavour, they spread out too much and didn't rise as high as we had hoped they would. We solved this problem by baking our loaves in metal pie plates, 20–22cm in diameter, lined with baking paper. You could also bake the round loaves in loose-bottomed baking tins about 20–23cm in diameter, with or without the removable bottom in place.

3 cups body-temperature water

5 tsp Surebake yeast

4 tsp salt

6½ cups (about 900g) high-grade white flour

Put the warm water in a large bowl. (The water is the right temperature if you shut your eyes and lower a finger or two into it, and don't notice the water feeling warm or cool.)

Sprinkle the yeast and salt over the liquid and stir until you can't feel any granules.

Using a fork, toss the flour in its large bag or container, then spoon or fork it into a cup measure, and tip one cupful of flour at a time, onto the yeast mixture. Don't pack or shake down the flour in the cup at any stage, or stir the flour into the liquid, until all the flour has been added.

Use a wooden spoon or a flexible stirrer to mix the flour and liquid together. It should form a soft, rather sticky ball when the flour is all mixed in.

Scrape down the sides of the bowl, cover the bowl with a plate or cling film, and leave the soft mixture to rise, and the top of the dough to level off. This could be 3–5 hours at room temperature, or overnight (or several days) in the refrigerator.

When you are ready to use part of the dough, turn the oven on to 220°C with a rack just above the middle.

Sift up to half a cup of extra flour over the top and edges of the risen dough. Tilt the bowl, using a stirrer to help the soft dough separate from the edges of the bowl.

Tilting the bowl and using a sharp knife or a metal dough cutter, cut off half the dough or the amount you want to cook straight away. Cover the rest of the dough and put it back in the refrigerator.

Coat the dough you are going to bake with extra flour. Don't knead the dough, but push the edges underneath, making a ball of dough which is smooth and floury on top, and is pinched together underneath. Read the second paragraph of this recipe introduction, and put the dough in a pie plate or cake tin, with the bottom and sides lined with baking paper.

Leave the dough to rise again in a warm place for about an hour.

Just before you are planning to put the loaf in the preheated oven, sift some more flour over it.

Run a very sharp knife under a cold tap, then across the loaf. Make a grid as if you were going to play noughts and crosses, or make three or four cuts in one direction only. You will see the cuts open up as you make them!

Put the bread in the oven (on a pre-heated ceramic tile if you have one). Bake the loaf at 220°C for about 30 minutes, until the top is fairly dark brown, then stand the loaf on a cooling rack until it is quite cold.

NOTE: This is not essential, but it is a good thing to do. Once you have made your dough, put a heavy cast iron frying pan two thirds of the way down the oven, before or while you heat the oven. After you have put the loaf in the oven to cook, pour about a cup of boiling water into the hot pan and shut the oven door quickly. The water will turn into steam as the bread cooks, helping it to rise, and making a crisp crust.

"No Knead" Baguettes

Baguettes are delicious, long, thin, crusty loaves, widely eaten in France.

We make our own very popular baguettes using the same easy "four ingredient" recipe that we use for our "round crusty loaves" on page 70. After you mix the dough, you can refrigerate it in a covered bowl for up to a week, using it as you like.

We make four long baguettes from the recipe on page 70 which uses about six cups of flour. Half the dough, made from three cups of flour, will make two baguettes, or if you prefer it, you may make one baguette and four or six smaller oval shaped rolls from the three cup dough (see details below.)

Although you can bake long baguettes on a flat oven tray, if you want evenly shaped, better looking baguettes, you may like to invest in a special baguette metal baking tray which, end on, looks like a W with three, rather than two "scoops". This baguette baking tray has little holes punched all over it, and also has a non-stick finish. These special baguette baking trays are stocked by some kitchen and bakeware specialty shops. (Check the price before you decide to buy one of these pans though, because they are not cheap!)

Measure and mix the 6-cup-of-flour-dough on page 70.

Leave it to stand at room temperature if you are planning to use half of it the same day, to bake one baguette plus 4–6 little rolls, or two baguettes and no rolls.

Leave the dough in its bowl, covered with cling film, at room temperature, to rise for 2–5 hours. Next, sprinkle some more flour over the dough, then tilt the bowl and tip out about half the dough, cutting it off with a sharp knife. Leave the other half, covering and refrigerating it to use during the next few days.

Cut the dough that is on your working surface in half, and gently shape it into two long thin rolls, each 38–40cm long, flouring them lightly.

If you want to bake two baguettes, put them on a baking tray or in two of the depressions in a baguette pan.

If you want to bake one baguette and 4–6 small rolls, cut one of the shaped baguettes diagonally into 4 or 6 small pieces.

Put the baguette and rolls on a baking tray OR if you have a baguette baking tray, put the baguette in one of the hollows, and two or three of the small rolls in each of the other two empty depressions, allowing space between them. Brush the baguette with water and make two or three long diagonal cuts in its top, with a very sharp knife.

Bake at 220°C for about 30 minutes until crusts are brown and crisp. These are best eaten within 24 hours, but may be reheated and eaten a day later, if necessary.

Easy "No Knead" Pizza

As long as you have the ingredients on hand, you will find that this is a really quick pizza to make! It takes only about 15 minutes to mix the dough, pat it into a circle, and put the toppings of your choice on it. Pop it into a very hot oven and let it cook for 15 minutes, while you tidy up the kitchen, then all you need to do is cut it in wedges and eat it! After you have made a few of these pizzas, you will probably decide that you can make them much more quickly and easily than going out to buy pizzas – and you will certainly save money!

For 1 pizza base, about 28cm across:

1 cup body-temperature water

1 tsp Surebake yeast

1 Tbsp olive oil

1 tsp salt

2 tsp sugar

2 cups (275g) high-grade white flour

About ¼ cup extra flour for coating

Turn the oven on to 250°C, with a rack above the middle of the oven, and a flat metal baking tray on it. (If you have a baking stone, put it in the oven instead of the metal tray.)

Measure the warm water into a fairly large bowl, and sprinkle in the yeast, oil, salt and sugar. Mix well until everything is evenly dispersed, then add the first measure of flour (spooning the flour lightly into the cup). Mix this to a soft dough with a wooden spoon or stirrer. The mixture should be soft and slightly sticky. Sprinkle a little of the extra flour over the yeast mixture in the bowl, and form it into a ball. Leave it to stand while you find and prepare your choice of topping ingredients. The dough will start to rise while you do this.

Place a large square of baking paper, or a large non-stick liner, on another flat metal baking tray.

Assemble your choice of pizza toppings. Use some or all of the following. The oil, tomatoes and cheese are usually regarded as essential. The others are optional.

Toppings:

Olive oil

Chopped tomatoes, seeds removed

Chopped canned anchovies, optional

Finely sliced small red onion, optional

Chopped bacon or ham, optional

about 1 cup of grated cheese

Sliced, pitted black olives, optional

Dried oregano, optional

Now work on the pizza crust. The dough should have risen slightly. Sprinkle some of the second measure of flour over the soft pizza dough. Use the stirrer to lift the floured dough away from the sides and bottom of the bowl, and turn it onto the centre of the baking paper or the non-stick liner.

With floury hands, first shape the floured dough into a ball, then, using your fingers and hands, pat the ball of dough out into a circle 30cm across, on the baking paper (or non-stick liner).

Drizzle a little olive oil on the dough and spread it fairly evenly with your fingers. Leaving the outer 2cm of the dough uncovered, sprinkle the chopped tomato over the pizza. Add pieces of anchovy if desired. Finely chop some red onion, coat it with a little extra oil and spread it on the pizza too. Add the chopped bacon or ham, then sprinkle the grated cheese over everything else. Place the sliced black olives on the cheese. Add the oregano or other herbs if you like. Fold the edges of the pizza in to make a 1cm rim. Drizzle a little more oil over the topping ingredients.

Turn the oven down to 225°C. Open the oven door and carefully slide the pizza, on its baking paper or liner, onto the heated pizza stone or the heated metal tray.

Bake for 15–20 minutes until the rim of the pizza is golden brown, then take it from the oven and slide the pizza off the baking paper or liner onto a cooling rack.

Cut into pieces with a knife, rotating cutter or kitchen scissors and eat while warm. Enjoy!

Small "No Knead" Round Bread Rolls

These little "no knead" rolls are really delicious! They have a nice round shape because they are baked in muffin pans. If left overnight the starter gives the bread a very nice sour dough flavour.

Starter:

½ cup lukewarm milk

¼ tsp Surebake yeast

½ cup high-grade (bread) flour (62g)

Dough:

½ cup water from the hot tap

2 Tbsp butter, at room temperature

½ cup milk (any type)

1 Tbsp instant active yeast

1 Tbsp sugar

1 egg

½ tsp salt

4½ cups (560g) high-grade (bread) flour

Semolina or cornmeal for coating

To make the starter, mix the milk and yeast together in a 2–3 cup lidded container. Add the flour and beat with a table fork until smooth, then leave the mixture, lightly covered, to stand in a warm (not hot) place, overnight, or for at least six hours. When ready to use, the mixture should be bubbling and smell slightly sour.

Make the dough the next morning, after checking that the starter is bubbling. Put the hot water in a large microwavable bowl, then add the room-temperature butter. Stir until the butter melts, then add the milk and the bubbling starter and mix well. Sprinkle the instant dried yeast over the surface and mix well until smooth.

Next add the sugar, egg and salt, and beat with a wooden spoon or silicone stirrer until everything is well mixed.

Add all the bread flour and beat again until the dough is smooth and satiny. If necessary, add more flour in tablespoon lots until the dough is just firm enough to turn out onto a floured board, pat out lightly, then fold in three, several times.

Put the dough in a clean, oiled bowl, then cover the bowl with cling film.

Shaping

For 12 small, round bread rolls cut the completed dough in half and refrigerate the half you are not using now for later use.

Put the dough you are using in a lightly oiled bowl and leave it to stand at room temperature for about an hour, until it is double its original size.

Turn the oven to 200°C with a rack above the middle.

Gently tip the risen dough onto a lightly floured board, without kneading or stretching it.

Using a dough cutter or an oiled chef's knife, cut the dough into halves, then quarters. Cut each quarter into three. Try to keep the pieces evenly sized.

Coat muffin pans (with depressions for 12 muffins/rolls) with non-stick spray or oil. Work with one piece of dough at a time. Make a circle, touching the tip of your thumb and forefinger together, then with your dominant hand, gently press the dough through the circle of your fingers. The smooth, stretched floured side of the dough will be the top of the roll, and the gathered edges should be pinched together at the bottom of the roll.

Gently put each roll in the muffin pan as it is shaped. Leave the rolls to rise to double their size.

Meantime, in a small pot or pan, mix 2 teaspoons cornflour with ½ cup of water. Heat stirring constantly until it boils, then leave to cool. Have about a tablespoon of rolled oats or poppy seeds handy if desired.

When the rolls are double their size, brush them gently with the cornflour mixture and sprinkle with the oats or seeds (if using). Bake at 200°C for about 10 minutes. Cool before lifting rolls from the pan onto a cooling rack.

"No Knead" Heavy Brown Loaf With Seeds

This recipe makes a heavy-textured, well-flavoured loaf which we bake in a large loaf tin which holds 10 cups (2.5 litres) of water. For preference, use a loaf tin with gently sloping sides, so the base is smaller than the top. The cooked loaf will have a fairly flat top, so you may want to turn it out of the pan, with the top of the loaf on the board, and the smaller base uppermost.

For a 1200–1300g loaf:

¼ cup each whole grain flaked oats, sunflower seeds, sesame seeds and linseeds

½ cup hot water

2 tsp of instant active yeast

2 cups lukewarm water

2 household Tbsp of golden syrup*

2 Tbsp canola or olive oil

4–5 cups (560–700g) wholemeal flour

2 tsp salt

*replace 1 Tbsp with molasses if available

Turn the oven to 190°C and put a rack just above the middle.

Prepare the mixed grains. Put oats and seeds in a fairly large, dry frying pan. Heat the pan, stirring and shaking it frequently, until the contents have browned lightly and have a "toasted" aroma. Take the pan off the stove and stir in the hot, but not boiling, water. Leave the mixture to stand until nearly all the water has been absorbed. (Drain off and discard any remaining liquid before adding the oats and seeds to the rest of the bread mixture.)

Put the yeast, lukewarm water, golden syrup (or syrup and molasses) and oil in a bowl or jug, and put this aside in a warm place for at least 10 minutes. The surface should have a film of fine bubbles on top by the end of this time.

While the yeast mixture stands, measure 4 cups of the flour and the salt into a large bowl.

Next, tip the yeast mixture and the room-temperature, drained seed mixture into the flour and salt. Stir well, preferably with a silicone stirrer or wooden spoon, until everything is evenly mixed. The mixture should be just too soft to knead, but not runny. If it is too wet, add up to a cup of the extra wholemeal flour, until the dough is just firm enough to form a cylinder which you

can hold on your flat hand and wrist. Gently tilt your hand and transfer the "sausage" of dough into the sprayed baking pan, held in your other hand. (If you jiggle the pan backwards and forwards, it should form an evenly shaped loaf, the length of the baking pan.) Add more flour while you do this, if necessary.

Cover the pan with cling film or stand it in a plastic bag, and leave it to rise in a warm place until the dough is almost double its size and has filled the loaf tin. This will probably take ½–1 hour.

Put the risen loaf into the preheated oven and bake it for about 40 minutes. (It is unlikely to rise more while it cooks.) The turned-out loaf should sound hollow when tapped. Cool it on a rack. When cold, wrap and refrigerate overnight. Slice it the next day, using a sharp serrated knife. (Use within three days, re-wrapping and refrigerating it between times.)

Baking Powder
BREAD

Irish Soda Bread

This couldn't actually be much quicker to make, and it's so good! Not surprisingly perhaps, it is a fairly dense loaf, but served warm from the oven (less than an hour from when you start mixing) with lashings of butter, it really is delicious.

For a 20cm round (900g) loaf:

3 cups (420g) standard plain flour

1½ tsp salt

1½ tsp sugar

1 tsp baking soda

1 tsp cream of tartar

195 m 1.

¾ cup milk

125

½ cup plain unsweetened yoghurt

310 gml.

Preheat the oven to 180°C.

Sift the flour, salt, sugar, baking soda and cream of tartar into a large bowl.

Measure the milk and yoghurt into a small bowl and stir to combine.

Pour the milk mixture into the dry ingredients and gently fold the mixture together, trying to combine it evenly but without over-mixing.

Tip the dough onto a lightly floured board and shape it into a ball. Flatten a little until it is disc-shaped and measures just over 15cm across and place it on a lightly floured or baking-paper lined baking sheet. Using a sharp knife, cut a deep cross (about halfway down) into the dough so it opens nicely during baking.

Bake in the middle of the oven at 180°C for 45–50 minutes or until golden brown and hollow sounding when tapped.

Date and Walnut Loaf

Here is a recipe for a date loaf that is easy to put together and bake, and which can be hidden in the refrigerator for a few days or frozen (useful if you like the idea of having a loaf hidden well away from members of your household who may well cut themselves so many "sampling" slices that there's no loaf left when you want it!) This recipe does in fact make two loaves, so you may decide to eat one and freeze the other.

For two medium-sized loaves:

2 cups good quality dates, pitted

1½ tsp salt

1½ cups sugar

¼ cup canola or other oil

3 large eggs

about 1 cup walnuts, finely chopped

3 cups (420g) self-raising flour

Optional Ingredients:

finely grated rind of a lemon or orange

1 tsp vanilla

2 tsp mixed spice

a few drops of orange oil

Preheat the oven to 180°C.

Put the dates in a pot large enough to mix all the ingredients. Add 3 cups water, bring to the boil and simmer for 4–5 minutes, squashing the dates and breaking them up. Turn off the heat as soon as the dates have broken up, then stand the pot in a sink of cold water to cool.

While the date mixture is still fairly hot, add the salt, sugar and oil and stir until the sugar dissolves. Add as many of the optional ingredients as you like. While you wait for the mixture to cool down further, break the eggs into a small bowl and beat with a fork or whisk until combined.

When the date mixture has cooled to room temperature, stir in the eggs and walnuts. Using a fork, stir the flour in its large container to aerate it before spooning the required amount into the date mixture. Fold, without stirring more than necessary, until no streaks of flour remain in the mixture.

Coat the insides of two loaf tins (each of which is 5–6 cup capacity) with non-stick spray. Spoon in the mixture, levelling the top of each.

Bake in the centre of the oven for 45–60 minutes or until a skewer poked into the centre of each loaf comes out clean.

Remove from the oven and cool on a rack, removing loaves from the tins only when they are firm enough to handle and keep their shape.

Serve slices lightly buttered or spread with cream cheese (mix a little finely grated orange or lemon peel through it for a change).

Cheesy Beer Bread

A friend of Simon's gave him this recipe years ago. Donn's recipe breaks so many of the traditional bread-making rules, it's hard to believe it works at all. Try it – it's delicious!

As it is a quick no-knead bread, containing no baker's yeast (unless you count the yeast content in the beer), it is not surprising that its appearance and texture are so different to 'normal' bread. Having said that, as long as you're not expecting a sandwich loaf, we think you'll be delighted with the results. A slice or two, warm from the oven, with a bowl of soup makes the perfect winter warmer.

Since this mixture contains little added fat, we expected it would go stale very quickly, but much to our surprise leftovers were surprisingly good when toasted.

For 1 loaf (4–6 servings):

3 cups (420g) self-raising flour

½ cup grated tasty cheese

1–2 Tbsp sugar

1 tsp salt

355ml can or bottle of beer

about 1 Tbsp of oil (optional)

Preheat the oven to 180°C.

Measure the flour into a large bowl. Spoon the flour from the bag into the measuring cup, rather than scooping it straight from the bag so it is not too densely packed – this can make a big difference to the total weight of flour used, as too much will make a dry loaf.

Add the grated cheese, sugar (use the larger quantity if using a dryish beer, and less if using a sweeter more malty beer). Toss together the dry ingredients to combine, then add the beer.

Stir everything together until the mixture looks more or less uniform and will hold together.

Oil or non-stick spray a 6–7 cup capacity loaf tin. Tip in the dough, roughly levelling the top. Brush the top with a little oil for more even browning, if you like, then place the loaf in the oven.

Bake for 45–60 minutes until the top is golden brown and the loaf sounds hollow when tapped. Remove from the oven and leave to cool for 10–15 minutes before slicing.

Brown Banana Loaf

This quick loaf has a good banana flavour, and may be sliced like a cake when fresh. For special occasions it is good spread with cream cheese flavoured with finely grated orange rind.

For a 23x10cm loaf:

100g butter

60 gms. ¾ cup sugar

1 egg

1 cup mashed ripe banana (use 2 medium-sized bananas)

1 cup (140g) wholemeal flour

¼ cup orange juice

¼–½ cup chopped walnuts

1 cup (140g) standard plain flour

1 tsp baking powder

1 tsp baking soda

Preheat the oven to 180°C.

Cream together the butter and sugar until light and fluffy. Add the egg and beat again. Add the mashed banana to the creamed mixture with the wholemeal flour, orange juice and walnuts. Stir together until just combined. Sift in the plain flour, baking powder and baking soda. Mix until all the ingredients are just combined.

Line the bottom and sides of a 23x10cm loaf tin with greaseproof paper and spoon in the mixture. Bake for about 1 hour. When the loaf is cooked, the centre will spring back when pressed, and a skewer poked into the middle will come out clean. Stand for 5–10 minutes before removing from the tin.

Store in a loosely covered container or refrigerate in a plastic bag.

lime juice + milk to texture

Date Scones

Alison's mother Margaret Payne (one of seven children brought up on a Canterbury farm) made truly wonderful scones – two or three batches a day, every Saturday and Sunday. Her scones were eaten hot from the oven, often as we sat on the front steps in the sun, drinking tea or glasses of milk, and chatting with family and friends. Margaret tried to teach Alison how to make scones but her recipe called for handfuls of flour, knobs of butter, and dashes of milk, and as Alison's hands were a different size, her scones were never much good! The following date scones are Alison's husband's favourites, and are made with standard measures. We hope they work well for you!

For 6 scones:

50g butter, melted

¾ cup milk

2 cups (260g) self-raising flour

1 tsp salt

1 Tbsp sugar

1 cup dates

Heat the oven to 210°C with a rack in or just above the middle.

Heat the butter in a microwave-proof container, or in a pot, until just melted, then add the milk. Put aside.

Toss/stir the flour with a fork to make sure it is not packed, then spoon it lightly into the cup, without shaking it. Put the two cups of flour in a bowl big enough to mix all the ingredients. Add the salt and sugar and toss well to mix.

Separate the dates if necessary and add to the flour mixture.

When the oven is up to heat, tip the slightly warm liquids into the dry ingredients all at once. Using a flat-bladed stirrer, fold the mixture together just until the dry ingredients are all dampened. Add extra milk if needed to make a soft moist ball of dough, then turn it out onto floured baking paper or a non-stick liner on an oven tray.

With floured hands, knead the ball of dough lightly, then pat it into a rectangle. Cut it lengthwise into two strips, then crosswise into three strips, making six scones altogether. Put the scones only 1cm apart, so the sides are soft rather than crusty, and bake for 10-15 minutes, until the tops are lightly browned.

Serve warm, split and buttered.

VARIATION: For plain scones, leave out the dates and mix and cook as above. Halve plain scones and top with raspberry jam and whipped cream.

Lemonade and Cream Scones

This isn't a traditional scone recipe, but it is so easy, good and reliable, we will probably never go back to Grandma's version. Once you've tried them, we think that you will probably agree.

Remember to stir the flour with a fork until light before measuring it, then spoon it into the measuring cup and level off the top without packing it down or banging it.

For 8 large square scones:

2 cups (280g) self-raising flour

¼ cup sugar

½ tsp salt

½ cup cream

½ cup lemonade plus 2 Tbsp extra

Preheat the oven to 230°C (220°C if using a fan oven).

Measure the dry ingredients into a large bowl. Toss together the dry ingredients, add the cream and all the lemonade and mix to make a soft dough.

Scrape the sides of the bowl and sprinkle enough extra flour over the ball of soft dough to allow you to turn it out onto a floured board and handle it without sticking.

Lightly knead the dough half a dozen times, then pat or roll out until it is about 2cm thick and twice as long as it is wide.

Using a floured knife to avoid sticking, cut the dough in half lengthwise, then in four crosswise.

Arrange the scones on a baking sheet (close together if you like soft sides, or further apart for crusty sides). For a good colour, brush the tops with a little milk or melted butter.

Bake for 10–12 minutes until the tops and bottoms are lightly browned.

Serve warm (or reheated), split, with butter and jam, or spread with jam and topped with whipped cream. If available, fresh strawberries or raspberries make an excellent addition.

NOTE: These scones stay fresh and soft for 48 hours → if they get the chance!

Gluten-free
BREAD

Gluten-free Bread Basics

These days, either by necessity or choice, an increasing number of people are adopting a gluten-free diet. Gluten is a protein, or more correctly a group of proteins, found in wheat (including spelt), rye, barley and triticale (a cross between wheat and barley). Oats were also regarded as containing gluten although this is now a matter of some conjecture and debate.

Unfortunately for bakers, gluten has some unique physical properties that make the dough elastic. There is no direct substitute for gluten. However, by using a combination of vegetable gums (guar or xanthan), eggs (or egg whites) and starches as we have here you can create a mixture (more a batter than a dough) that will hold the gas bubbles as the yeast acts and sets much the same way a 'conventional' dough does when baked. More importantly, the resulting bread tastes great and has a similar, although not identical, texture to 'normal' bread.

*Available on most newer machines. Unfortunately the 'Normal' cycles on bread machines give the dough a brief stir (or 'knock down') just before baking and this tends to knock the gas right out of a gluten-free mix.

We're delighted with the way these gluten-free breads look and taste, but they can be a little temperamental. We've found they work well in bread machines that have a gluten-free cycle* or when made in a cake mixer. They do seem particularly sensitive to the amount of water added, and small changes can have a significant effect on the size and shape of the loaves. If your loaves rise then collapse in the middle (or just have a very flat top) try adding 1 tablespoon less water next time. If your loaves are small, try adding 1 tablespoon more water.

Gluten-free Bread

Although this isn't exactly like a wheat-based bread, we think it's pretty close. The flavour and texture are good and it can be used for sandwiches and/or toast just as you would regular bread – and it's easy to make in a bread machine (although it must have a 'gluten-free' cycle) or using a mixer.

This mixture is very sensitive to the amount of water you add – you may have to vary the amount a little. We found we actually got a bigger loaf when we added a tablespoon or so more, but then the top of the loaf sometimes collapsed a little as it baked.

For a 750g loaf:

2 tsp instant active yeast

1 cup warm water plus 2 Tbsp extra

3 tsp sugar

1½ tsp salt

3 tsp guar gum (see page 91)

1 large egg plus 1 large egg white

¼ cup skim milk powder

3 Tbsp canola oil

½ cup (65g) chickpea flour*

½ cup (65g) tapioca starch*

1 cup (140g) rice flour*

1 cup (150g) maize cornflour*

*Replace this with 3 cups of our gluten-free flour mix (page 84) if you like.

Bread Machine Instructions
Carefully measure all the ingredients into a 750g capacity bread machine. For the most effective mixing, it is best to add the liquids first.

Set to the GLUTEN FREE bread cycle, MEDIUM crust and START. Because of the egg content, this isn't a good timer/time delay bread.

Hand-made Bread Instructions
Measure the yeast, water, sugar and salt into the bowl of a heavy-duty mixer and leave to stand for 5 minutes.

Sprinkle in the guar gum (do this gradually to avoid it forming lumps), then add the egg and egg white and the milk powder. Beat on a medium-high speed for 2 minutes until the mixture looks foamy.

Add the oil and flours, then mix again at medium speed for 2 minutes, stopping and scraping down the sides of the bowl after about 1 minute.

Thoroughly coat the inside of a large (7–8 cup capacity) loaf tin with non-stick spray, then pour/spoon the batter into it. Spread the batter evenly in the tin and smooth the top with an oiled spatula.

Put the tin in a warm place to rise (see page 9) for 50–60 minutes or until the mixture has reached to the top of the tin (keep an eye on it because if it rises over the top it will spill down the sides).

Bake at 200°C for 15–20 minutes until golden brown and hollow sounding when tapped. Remove from the oven and cool in the tin for a few minutes before tipping onto a rack to cool completely.

NOTE: Once you have our basic recipe worked out, you might like to try adding a few of your own 'extras'. You can add about ¼ cup (total) seeds or gluten-free grains (poppy, sesame, sunflower or even soaked and drained soy kibble) etc. to the basic loaf to vary the flavour, texture and appearance of the bread if you like.

Gluten-free Fruit and Nut Loaf

Nothing beats the smell of a spicy bread baking (well, maybe the smell of it being toasted) – and this is no exception. We are particularly pleased with the way this bread turns out – we think eaters of this bread would never know it was gluten-free unless they were told.

For a 1kg loaf:

2 tsp instant active yeast

1 cup plus 2 Tbsp warm water

2 Tbsp sugar

1½ tsp salt

50g butter, softened

3 tsp guar gum (see page 91)

2 large eggs

¼ cup skim milk powder

½ cup (55g) chickpea flour*

1½ cups (190g) tapioca starch*

1 cup (150g) maize cornflour*

¼ cup brown sugar

2 tsp ground cinnamon

½ tsp ground mixed spice

½ cup each sultanas and walnut pieces

Bread Machine Instructions

Carefully measure all the ingredients into a 750g capacity bread machine. For the most effective mixing, it is best to add the liquids first.

Set to the GLUTEN FREE bread cycle, MEDIUM crust and START. Because of the egg content this isn't a good timer/time delay bread.

Hand-made Bread Instructions

Measure the yeast, water, first measure of sugar, the salt and butter into the bowl of a heavy-duty mixer and leave to stand for 5 minutes.

Sprinkle in the guar gum (do this gradually to avoid it forming lumps), then add the egg and egg white and the milk powder. Beat on a medium-high speed for 2 minutes until the mixture looks foamy.

Add flours, brown sugar, spices, sultanas and nuts, then mix again at medium speed for 2 minutes, stopping and scraping down the sides of the bowl after about 1 minute.

Thoroughly coat the inside of a large (7–8 cup capacity) loaf tin with non-stick spray, then pour/spoon the batter into it. Spread the batter evenly in the tin and smooth the top with an oiled spatula.

Put the tin in a warm place to rise (page 9) for 50–60 minutes or until the mixture has reached to top of the tin (keep an eye on it because if it rises over the top it will spill down the sides).

Bake at 200°C for 15–20 minutes until golden brown and hollow sounding when tapped. Remove from the oven and cool in the tin for a few minutes before tipping onto a rack to cool completely.

*You can use 3 cups of the gluten-free flour mix (below) instead of this combination, but it will probably result in a slightly smaller loaf.

Gluten-free Flour Mix

There aren't so many ingredients that it's impossible or impractical to measure out everything in this mixture on a loaf-by-loaf basis, but if you know you are going to be making gluten-free bread on a regular basis, it really is much simpler to have the base mixture premade.

It is important that everything is evenly mixed. If you use a tight-sealing canister or container (you will need one that holds about 5 litres), you can shake and/or roll it to help combine everything.

For a 12-cup mix (enough for 4 loaves)

2 cups (250g) chickpea flour

2 cups (250g) tapioca starch

4 cups (600g) maize cornflour

4 cups (560g) rice flour

Measure the chickpea flour and tapioca starch into a large bowl or canister. Using a wire whisk, thoroughly stir the mixture, making sure you are getting into any edges or corners. If using a canister (see introduction), put on the lid and give it a good shake.

Add the maize cornflour, and repeat the mixing process, then add the rice flour and repeat the mixing process.

Store in an air-tight container until required.

Gluten-free Ciabatta, Buns or Pizza Base

Unlike other gluten-free breads that are made from a mixture more like a batter than a dough, this one is made from a much stiffer mixture which can be shaped a bit more like a traditional dough. The resulting bread has quite a fine and interesting chewy texture. While this dough has a similar consistency to a standard dough, it is different to handle – because it's quite sticky and not really elastic like a conventional dough it is best just patted into shape with well-oiled hands.

For 1 ciabatta-style loaf, 6 buns or one large pizza base

½ cup warm water

2 tsp instant active yeast

2 tsp sugar

1 tsp salt

3 tsp guar gum (page 91)

1 Tbsp canola oil

2 egg whites

1 cup (125g) tapioca starch

1 cup (140g) rice flour

¼ cup skim milk powder

up to ¼ cup warm water

Bread Machine Instructions

Measure all the ingredients, including the extra water, into the bread machine. Set to the DOUGH cycle and press START. Check the dough after 5 minutes of mixing and scrape any unmixed flour off the sides. Stop the machine 30 minutes after mixing has started and shape and bake as below.

Hand-made Bread Instructions

Measure the warm water, yeast, sugar and salt into the bowl of a heavy-duty mixer. Leave to stand for 5 minutes, then sprinkle in the guar gum and add the egg whites. Beat at medium speed for 2–3 minutes or until the mixture is pale and slightly foamy looking.

Measure in the flours and milk powder, then mix on medium speed until the mixture begins to bind together. Add as much of the extra water as is required to form a cohesive dough, then mix for 2–3 minutes longer.

Shaping and Baking

Thoroughly oil your hands, and lightly oil a baking sheet (or baking paper-lined baking tray). Tip/scrape the dough from the mixing bowl or bread machine onto the oiled surface. Lightly sprinkle or spray the dough with oil.

Pizza

Gently pat out the dough into an oval shape about 25x35cm of about 5–7mm thickness (it's quite easy to tear the dough so avoid pulling it – placing a sheet of baking paper on top of the dough may make this easier). Allow to rise for 5–10 minutes, then top and bake as described on page 22.

Bread or Buns

Pat the dough into a 25–30cm long and 5–6cm thick sausage shape and leave intact for a single loaf. To make buns use an oiled knife to cut the dough into six equal portions, then use well-oiled hands to shape them into balls.

Arrange the loaf or balls on the oiled baking sheet (leaving 10cm between the buns), then leave to rise in a warm place for about 1 hour.

Bake at 200°C until golden brown and hollow sounding when tapped, about 10–12 minutes for buns or 12–15 minutes for the loaf.

Bread glazes and toppings

What you put on the surface of home-made bread affects its appearance a lot.

Floury-topped Breads

A floury top gives a "cottagey" home-baked look to a loaf or rolls. Sprinkle the flour using a shaker with small holes – or a sieve – on the risen loaf. If you lightly wet the surface first, the flour sticks better, and the crust tends to be firmer.

If you score the crust of the risen loaf with a very sharp blade after flouring it, but before baking it, the cuts will make an attractive contrast to the texture and colour.

Egg Glaze for Breads

If you brush the surface of the risen loaf with an egg glaze just before it is baked, it will brown better and have an attractive shine. The crust will be thin and fairly tender.

Shake together in a tightly closed jar or beat with a fork in a bowl:

1 egg

1 Tbsp water

½ tsp sugar

This glaze will keep in the refrigerator for 2–3 days.

For more shine, brush on extra glaze after cooking while the bread is still very hot.

An egg glaze allows a topping to stick better, too. Brush the uncooked bread with the glaze, then sprinkle with poppy seeds, sesame seeds, sunflower or pumpkin seeds, coarse cornmeal, etc.

NOTE: kibbled grains harden during cooking – take care so you don't break a tooth!

Milk-glazed Breads

For a slightly glazed appearance and a thin crust, brush the bread with milk instead of egg glaze. Milk containing some fat works better than very low-fat milk.

Water and Steam

For a crusty loaf, put a roasting dish containing 1cm water on the bottom shelf of the oven 5 minutes before you put the bread in. For extra crustiness, spray the crust with water several times during cooking. Remove the dish with the water 5 minutes before you take the bread from the oven. Spraying by itself, without the pan of water in the oven, is not particularly effective.

A longer cooking time produces a crustier loaf, but you must be careful not to overcook the bread.

Golden Syrup Glaze

To give a shiny brown glaze to sweet buns and bread, make a syrup by bringing to the boil 1 tablespoon each golden syrup, honey and water. Brush on buns and breads (which have not been egg-glazed) as soon as they come out of the oven. This glaze softens the crust, too.

For a darker-coloured glaze, replace the honey with extra syrup. For a lighter coloured glaze, use all honey and no syrup.

87

Shaping bread dough

Bread dough may be shaped in many ways to make loaves, rolls or a variety of other shapes.

In the individual recipes in this book, we have given suggestions for shaping each quantity of dough in only a few ways.

Initially we hope that you will make a number of the breads, following our instructions precisely, until you feel comfortable working with bread dough.

Once you have reached this stage we are sure that you will be ready to have fun shaping dough in other ways.

We have compiled the following useful list so that you can look up the shaping details on the pages listed, then use the instructions to shape whatever dough you have made by hand or in a bread machine.

There are, however, two very wet doughs that we do not recommend shaping in other ways. The first of these is ciabatta (page 34), which is wonderful just the way it is, and will lose its character if you change it. Heavy multigrain bread (page 15), the second of these, is too wet to knead and shape by hand, but you can add more flour until it is firm enough to shape as you like. The resulting dough will make a lighter, more open-textured bread than the original recipe.

Shaping guide

Rectangular tinned loaf, see page 11 and subsequent pages.

Muffin buns, see page 12. Make sure you spray the pans well so they don't stick.

Monkey bread, see page 12. Monkey bread is easy to pull apart. You can make your own variations using strips of dough instead of balls. Bake in well-oiled or buttered loaf tins, ring pans, or in muffin pans. Have fun!

Round loaf, see page 28. We usually put our round loaves in a large round cake pan, just in case they spread more than we want them to as the dough rises and bakes. You don't have to do this, though.

Round bread rolls, see page 21

Long rolls, see page 21

Hamburger buns, see page 21

Hot dog buns, see page 21

Pizza, see page 22

Pita bread, see page 22

Breadsticks, see page 24

Pinwheels, see pages 25 and 64

Filled long loaf, see page 25

Calzone (folded pizza), see page 25

Focaccia shaping, see pages 28, 31

Crostini, see page 33

French bread shape, see page 37

Cottage loaf, see page 39

Braided loaf, see page 40

Checker-board topped loaf, see page 44

Oval free-standing loaves, see page 44

Rolled triangles, roll dough thinly, brush with butter, and cut into triangles. Enclose a filling before rolling up, see page 53.

Rolled "snails" see page 54

Soft-sided buns, see page 61

Ring, see page 63. OR snip a long filled roll part way through, at 3cm intervals, and join the ends to form a ring (have the snipped part outermost). Twist cut pieces so they lie flat on the baking sheet.

Filled braid, see page 66

Flat breads, see page 22

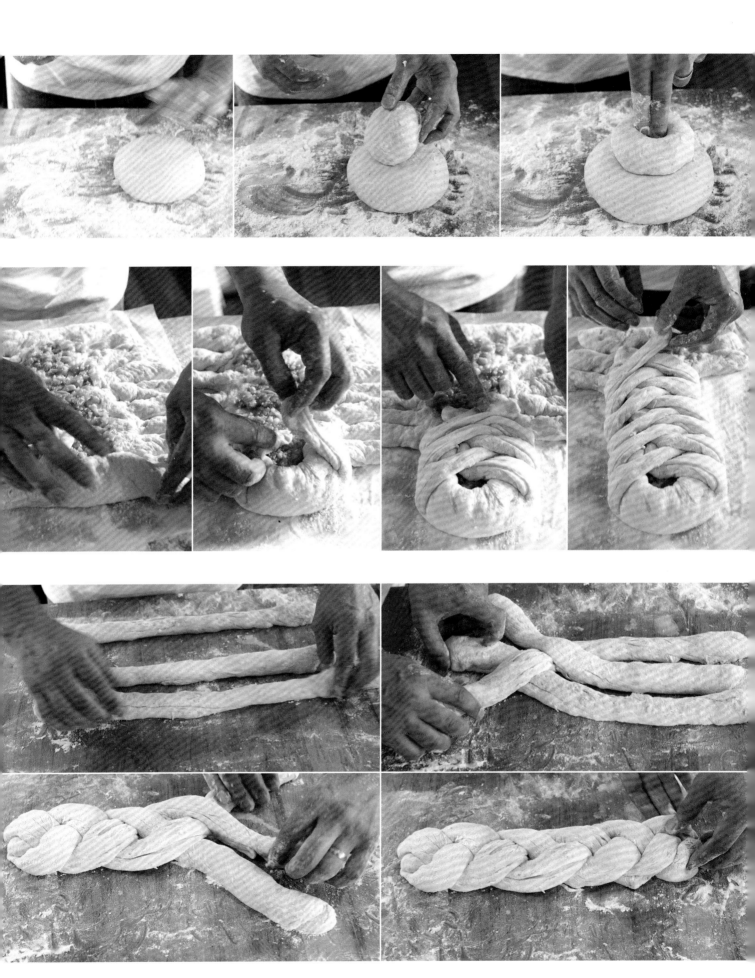

Flour and other ingredients

Flour Basics

Whole wheat is the basic raw material for all flour production. Wheat seeds, sometimes called wheat berries, consist of tough bran layers surrounding the starchy white endosperm, and at the blunt ends the yellowish embryos or germ. High in fibre, whole wheat can be soaked and used in grain breads, but is more commonly used in its kibbled form (see next page). Soak or boil before adding to dough.

White Flour

During the process of milling, the starchy white inner part (endosperm) is separated from the bran and germ, then crushed to give flour. Unfortunately this process removes a considerable amount of fibre (from the bran) and vitamins (from the bran and germ), but effectively increases the proportions of starch and protein which are essential for the manufacture of good bread.

Most retail outlets offer two types of white flour (excluding self-raising): high-grade flour (sometimes called bread flour or baker's flour) and standard plain flour.

High Grade or **Bread Flour** is used for most recipes in this book and has a higher protein content, making it stronger than standard plain flour, and particularly suitable for use in bread.

Standard Plain Flour with its lower protein content is more suitable for most other general baking (cakes, biscuits, etc.), but is occasionally used in bread where a soft or light product is desired.

Wholemeal Flour is literally the product produced when the whole wheat grain is crushed into flour. Wholemeal flour is much higher in fibre and some vitamins than white flour. In practice, stoneground wholemeal flours are made this way, but large modern flour mills tend to separate the bran, germ and endosperm at an early stage, and then recombine them in proportions that result in the wholemeal flour we know.

As wholemeal flours contain the germ, which is relatively rich in oils*, they will go rancid in time. To avoid this happening, keep your wholemeal flour in a cool dark place and buy quantities that you can use within 4–6 weeks. If you have the space, consider storing wholemeal flour in the refrigerator or freezer, but remember to allow it to return to room temperature before use.

The presence of the bran effectively dilutes the gluten proteins present. It provides additional weight for the gluten network formed in the dough to support. For this reason, loaves made solely (or with high proportions) of wholemeal flour will rise less and be more dense than those made with white flour. For best results don't use more than a 50/50 wholemeal to white flour ratio. If substituting wholemeal for white flour, remember to increase the water content by 1–2 tablespoons per cup of wholemeal used, as the bran also absorbs more water. It may also be worth adding 1–2 teaspoons of gluten per cup of wholemeal used.

*The stonegrinding process distributes these oils differently in the flour, which can affect baking quality – some bread machine makers suggest avoiding its use.

Organic Flour is available, but may vary in bread-making quality. The amount of organic wheat grown is not large, so millers may not be as selective with the raw material as they are with conventionally farmed wheat.

Bran (Wheat Bran) is the protective outer layer of the wheat grain that is removed during the milling of white flour. It is a very good source of fibre and relatively high in vitamins and minerals, but contains no gluten-forming proteins. Best added sparingly (1–2 tablespoons per loaf) as the additional weight (for the gluten to hold) will decrease the size of loaves. Add a little extra additional water when adding extra bran to bread.

Buckwheat Flour comes from a plant, not a grass, and must be threshed before being ground to remove the inedible outer husk. It contains no gluten. Add sparingly to bread for its nutty flavour.

Bulgar (or Burghul) is kibbled wheat that has been cooked and dried. In theory it can be added to bread dough unsoaked (but you will need to add more water as well).

Corn Meal may vary in size from a fine yellow powder to coarse yellow chunks. It contains no gluten so will not form a dough as wheat flour does. Add in small proportions for texture and/or visual appeal.

Gluten or **Gluten Flour** (sometimes called Vital Wheat Gluten) is a collective term for the dough-forming proteins of wheat. It is the gluten that gives bread dough its strength and, most importantly, its elasticity (the ability to form an elastic dough is unique to wheat).

Gluten flour is prepared by washing the starch out of dough, then drying and grinding the sticky mass of protein left behind.

To some extent, adding additional gluten to a dough will increase the size of loaves (particularly true for those with high proportions of wholemeal or whole grains). However, adding gluten also increases the amount of work that must be put into dough to produce good bread, and this translates into longer kneading or mixing times. As bread machines mix for fixed periods of time, if there is too much gluten present the dough will not fully develop in the time allowed, and there may be no improvement in the finished loaf.

Guar Gum is made from the endosperm of the seed of the legume Cyamopsis tetragonolobus, an annual plant grown in arid regions of India that works well as an economical thickener and stabiliser. Because it can form a thick sticky gel when mixed with water it is useful in helping to create gluten free bread and doughs. Xanthan gum can be used in the same way (and quantities) but it is more expensive.

Kibble Mix (Cereal Mix) is a pre-prepared mixture of kibbled grains used by bakeries. Not usually available from supermarkets, it may be obtained from flour mills. It often looks more interesting than standard kibbled grains, as the mill may add coloured (purple) wheat, which is a specialty of New Zealand.

Kibbled Rye is coarsely chopped whole rye grains added to bread for flavour, texture and additional fibre. It should be soaked or boiled before use in bread.

Kibbled Wheat comprises coarsely chopped wheat grains, a good source of fibre and texture. It should be soaked or boiled before being added to the dough.

Lecithin Granules are a natural emulsifier produced from soya beans. Emulsifiers improve the consistency and performance of doughs as well as slowing the staling process. Lecithin granules may be used in place of non-emulsifying fats such as oil or butter in most recipes, and have the additional advantage of being lower in calories on a volume for volume basis.

Rye Flour is produced from the starchy endosperm of the rye grain in much the same way as white flour. It may vary from quite light in colour to quite dark, depending on the extraction rate (how hard the bran is scraped) during milling. It may be used to replace wheat flour in part, and is very common in northern European bread.

Rye Meal (rye meal flour) is a fine floury meal produced by grinding whole rye grains. Rye does contain some gluten protein but not as much as wheat. It may be used in place of some wheat flour (don't replace more than a third), but will tend to result in a denser, more solid loaf.

Rolled Oats are whole oats that have been steamed, then rolled flat. Add in small quantities for flavour, texture and added fibre. Rolled oats hold water, so bread made with them goes stale more slowly.

Soya Flour is made from ground soya beans and is a good source of additional proteins, complementing those in wheat. It may be added in small quantities but if you add too much you will get a distinctive "beany" flavour.

Wheat germ is the embryo of the wheat seed. If the seed is allowed to sprout it is the germ that will grow into the new plant, drawing food from the starchy endosperm. Although high in non-gluten proteins, oils, B vitamins, vitamin E and minerals, unfortunately wheat germ does little for baking quality. However, adding 1–2 tablespoons per loaf will boost the nutritive value of your bread without affecting quality too much.

Yeast: we have used two types of yeast in this book, Active Dried Yeast and Surebake Yeast. Active Dried Yeast is an all-purpose yeast that may be used for processes other than bread making, e.g. brewing. Surebake yeast has been formulated especially for bread making and in most situations produces better bread.

Remember that yeast is a living organism (and has a finite shelf life, check the expiry date from time to time) and should be kept in the refrigerator. High temperatures used too early in the bread-making process will kill the yeast so the bread will not rise. On the other hand, if the dough is too cool, the bread will rise very slowly (occasionally this is desirable).

Surebake yeast   Instant active yeast

Weights and measures

When you make bread by hand, exact flour and liquid measurements are not as important as they are in much other baking. This is because you work by feel, adding extra flour as it is needed. For this reason, the exact amount you use may differ with each batch of flour you buy.

When you make bread in a bread machine it is much more important to measure accurately, then to adjust the wetness or dryness of the dough as the machine kneads it (page 4).

Take care when measuring yeast, salt and sugar, since small variations in amounts may affect your dough considerably.

Use level metric 250ml cups and metric measuring spoons unless the recipe specifies otherwise: 1 tablespoon (Tbsp) measures 15ml, and 1 teaspoon (tsp) 5ml. For ease and speed we use single capacity measuring cups for quarter and half-cup quantities.

NOTE: an Australian tablespoon = 20ml or 4 teaspoons

When measuring liquids, fill the containers brimming full.

Small amounts of butter are measured by volume: 1 teaspoon weighs 5g and 1 tablespoon weighs about 15g.

When measuring the flour, stir the flour near the top of the storage container, then scoop it lightly into the measuring cup without packing, tapping or shaking the cup, and level the top. When measured in this way, 1 cup of bread/high quality/baker's flour weighs 135–140g.

It is easy, even for experienced cooks, to leave out an ingredient every now and then. Leaving out (or doubling up on) yeast, salt or sugar can ruin your bread, so take extra care! We find it best to line up all the ingredients in the recipe, check that the line-up is complete, then measure each ingredient into the bowl, putting its container away or aside (well away so you won't accidentally use it again). Then, before going on to the next step, check to make sure you have not left melted butter or warmed liquid in the microwave oven – all too easy to do!

Conversions

for different capacity bread machines

Most modern bread machines make 750g (using 3 cups of flour) or 1kg (using 4 cups of flour) loaves. We have given quantities suitable for 750g machines, however these will also work fine in 1kg machines, although you can scale up our recipes using the table below if you want. Some older bread machines are designed to make a 500g (1lb) loaf using about 2 cups flour. If you have one of these machines, do not overload it, but simply use two-thirds of the quantities given in our recipes. The table below gives approximate scaled-down quantities of the commonly used measures.

1kg Machines	750g Machines	500g Machines
1½ tsp	1 tsp	scant ¾ tsp
3 tsp	2 tsp	1½ tsp
4 tsp	3 tsp	2 tsp
4 tsp	1 Tbsp	2 tsp
2 Tbsp plus 2 tsp	2 Tbsp	1 Tbsp plus 1 tsp
4 Tbsp	3 Tbsp	2 Tbsp
¼ cup plus 4 tsp	¼ cup	2 Tbsp plus 2 tsp
½ cup plus 2 Tbsp	½ cup	¼ cup plus 1 Tbsp
1 cup	¾ cup	½ cup
1¼ cups plus 1 Tbsp	1 cup	½ cup plus 2 Tbsp
1½ cups	1¼ cup	½ cup plus 2 Tbsp
2 cups	1½ cups	1 cup
2½ cups plus 2 Tbsp	2 cups	1¼ cups plus 1 Tbsp
3 cups	2½ cups	1½ cups plus 3 Tbsp
4 cups	3 cups	2 cups
2 small eggs	1 large egg	1 small egg

Remember to check the dough after a few minutes of mixing. It should have formed a smooth-looking ball or cylinder. If it is too wet, add 1 tablespoon of flour, if too dry add 2 teaspoons of water. Repeat until the dough is the right consistency.

Index

Knives etc., by Mail Order

For about 20 years Alison has imported her favourite, very sharp kitchen knives from Switzerland. They keep their edges well, are easy to sharpen, a pleasure to use, and make excellent gifts.

VEGETABLE KNIFE $8.00

Ideal for cutting and peeling vegetables, these knives have a straight edged 85mm blade and black (dishwasher-proof) nylon handle. Each knife comes in an individual plastic sheath.

BONING/UTILITY KNIFE $9.50

Excellent for boning chicken and other meats, and/or for general kitchen duties. Featuring a 103mm blade that curves to a point and a dishwasher-proof, black nylon handle. Each knife comes in a plastic sheath.

SERRATED KNIFE $9.50

These knives are unbelievably useful. They are perfect for cutting cooked meats, ripe fruit and vegetables, and slicing bread and baking. Treated carefully, these blades stay sharp for years. The serrated 110mm blade is rounded at the end with a black (dishwasher-proof) nylon handle and each knife comes in an individual plastic sheath.

THREE-PIECE SET $22.00

This three-piece set includes a vegetable knife, a serrated knife (as described above) and a right-handed potato peeler with a matching black handle, presented in a white plastic wallet.

GIFT BOXED KNIFE SET $44.00

This set contains five knives plus a matching right-handed potato peeler. There is a straight bladed vegetable knife and a serrated knife (as above), as well as a handy 85mm serrated blade vegetable knife, a small (85mm) utility knife with a pointed tip and a smaller (85mm) serrated knife. These elegantly presented sets make ideal gifts.

SERRATED CARVING KNIFE $28.50

This fabulous knife cuts beautifully and is a pleasure to use; it's ideal for carving or cutting fresh bread. The 21cm serrated blade does not require sharpening. Once again the knife has a black moulded, dishwasher safe handle and comes in a plastic sheath.

COOK'S KNIFE $35.00

An excellent all-purpose kitchen knife. With a well balanced 19cm wedge-shaped blade and a contoured black nylon handle, these knives make short work of slicing and chopping, and have come out on top of their class in several comparative tests. Each dishwasher-safe knife comes with its own plastic sheath.

VICTORINOX MULTIPURPOSE KITCHEN SHEARS $29.50

Every kitchen should have a pair of these! With their comfortable nylon handles and sharp blades these quality shears make short work of everything from cutting a piece of string or sheet of paper to jointing a whole chicken. Note: Black handle only.

STEEL $20.00

These steels have a 20cm 'blade' and measure 33cm in total. With its matching black handle the steel is an ideal companion for your own knives, or as a gift. Alison gets excellent results using these steels. N.B. Not for use with serrated knives.

PROBUS SPREADER/SCRAPER $7.50

After her knives, these are the most used tools in Alison's kitchen! With a comfortable plastic handle, metal shank and flexible plastic blade (suitable for use on non-stick surfaces), these are excellent for mixing muffin batters, stirring and scraping bowls, spreading icings, turning pikelets etc., etc...

NON-STICK LINERS

Re-usable SureBrand PTFE non-stick liners are another essential kitchen item – they really help avoid the frustration of stuck-on baking, roasting or frying. Once you've used them, you'll wonder how you did without!

Round tin liner	(for 15-23cm tins)	$6.50
	(for 23-30cm tins)	$9.50
Square tin liner	(for 15-23cm tins)	$6.50
	(for 23-30cm tins)	$9.50
Ring tin liner	(for 23cm tins)	$6.95
Baking sheet liner	(33x44cm)	$13.95
Barbeque liner	(Heavy duty 33x44cm)	$17.95
Frypan liner	(Heavy duty round 30cm)	$10.95

All prices include GST. Prices current at time of publishing, subject to change without notice. Please add $5.00 post & packing to any order (any number of items).

Make cheques payable to Alison Holst Mail Orders and post to:

Alison Holst Mail Orders
FREEPOST 124807
PO Box 17016
Wellington

Or visit us at www.holst.co.nz